Read what people *just like you* are saying about

PROFILES IN
DENTAL COURAGE

"As a teacher of young children, one of my primary responsibilities is to teach them to be thoughtful and effective writers. A strategy I always teach them is to "hook the reader" with an intriguing or interesting title and/or lead sentence. The title of your book, "Profiles in Dental Courage" certainly accomplishes that. The reference to JFK is both appropriate and assures that many readers will want to immediately delve into the book. Of course, as one of your patients, I just knew the book would be all the things it is- funny, interesting, helpful, and well written. It has so many excellent elements, including, but not limited to excellent tips, interesting and poignant stories, and powerful photographs. I will admit I read through the book quickly, but it is definitely a book I will reread for a few reasons. It serves as a reference tool for maintaining healthy teeth, it serves as a source of inspiring stories, and it serves as a source of thought provoking quotes, many of which I might reference in my own writing. Thank you for adding an important book to my library."

Gina James, New York

"If there's a prescription for painless dentistry, perhaps Dr. Passes and his team have come close to discovering it. As evident in the pages of "Profiles in Dental Courage," Passes Dental provides patients with an abundance of compassion coupled with state of the art dentistry. Patients are given what they need to help them manage their fears. Personally, I've learned the best way to deal with fear is to go through it. Somehow it's not as frightening looking back from the other side. Thank you Dr. Passes and your supportive team for helping me find my way to the other side."

Jill Oliver, New York

"I walked into Dr. Passes' office like I walked into many dentist offices before, with a feeling of sickness in my stomach, and knowing that I would eventually run out. For the last decade, I would show up for my yearly dentist visit and leave the office without even being treated. My teeth were to the point of not being able to chew food anymore. I was in pain, but my fear of being treated by a dentist was greater than any cavity's pain. Every time I sat in a dentist chair I got the same judgmental look, followed by a harsh speech, – "How did you get it this bad? It wasn't until I met Dr. Passes that everything changed. His first question was "how can I serve you?" I immediately felt his empathy. He listened and understood my fear. He explained what was wrong with my teeth, and how he was going to fix them without any pain.

Dr. Passes deeply understands why some patients have dentist phobia, and he is able to take them from phobia to courage in a single visit. He is a miracle worker. He is a remarkable human being with ability to understand people, and help them move from fear to empowerment. This book is about how you too can move from fear to empowerment. It is full of great stories – he also happens to be a gifted storyteller – providing tips on how by taking care of your teeth, your entire life could be transformed for the better.

This book is also an introduction to a new kind of dentist, a dentist of the future because Dr. Passes is a pioneer in his field. He has invented and worked with advanced technology, and is also a doctor who creates amazing experiences in one visit. At his office he sings, tells stories, and creates an environment where patients feel safe and well taken care of, and where nothing happens at random, everything is carefully studied and applied with the utmost care and thoughtfulness."

Daniel De Blois, New York

"If you or anyone you know are phobic about a trip to the dentist, READ THIS BOOK. It is by turns innovative, instructive and inspirational. Dr. Passes has pioneered and perfected modern stress free dentistry. You owe it to yourself to read and absorb the contents of this book. Then contact Dr. Passes."

Brad Winslow, New York

"It all started over 30 years ago, when my husband Gene was a New York City police officer and Dr. Passes's office was on his patrol beat. He kept talking about this wonderful young dentist he was going to and so I also became a patient and the rest is history. Dr. Passes is so professional and caring, but he is also very funny and he uses his comic side and musical ability to calm the most anxious patient—Me!"

Kathy Leonard, New York

"What a cool book. I learned a lot about Dr. Passes and his journey in the field of dentistry. A must read for anyone with anxiety about seeing a dentist. An insightful book that not only reveals how painless dentistry is today, but also how committed and compassionate Dr. Passes is about pain management and making sure your dental experience is all about you and your needs!."

Maryanne Fitch, New York

PROFILES IN DENTAL COURAGE

How to Completely Overcome
Your Fear of the Dentist

HARVEY PASSES DDS

Published by Success, Ltd.

ISBN: 0984649611
ISBN-13: 9780984649617
Library of Congress Control Number: 2014907494
TechnoMagic Publications - Manhasset, NY

To order additional copies of *Profiles in Dental Courage,*
please contact Passes Dental Care, 415 Northern Boulevard, Great Neck, NY 11021.

Call 1-516-858-5921, or write to passes@optonline.net.

DEDICATION

This publication is dedicated to the more than one hundred million people who avoid dental treatment because of dental anxiety. It is committed to those who suffer from their own dental neglect because they cannot cope with sitting in the dental chair. It is written for those millions of people who will needlessly receive false teeth this year, because they were afraid to seek routine care in previous years. It is to avoid these preventable negative consequences that I have devoted my energy, time, and career. It is my sincerest belief that *Profiles in Dental Courage* will be "a ray of sunshine through the turbulent storm of dental anxiety."

TABLE OF CONTENTS

Welcome to Your New Beginning

Fear stinks. It can freeze you dead in your tracks. It can fool you into making the wrong decisions. It is true that appropriate fear can save your life by having you run away from danger. But misperceived fear without basis can make an illusion become your reality. After all, perception is reality. Think of those moments, in the dead of night, alone in your home, when that slightest sound froze your movements. Or the apprehension you experience when you think about your next dental visit being a repeat of the last bad one. Something usually triggers that fear, and when it begins, you live with it. It's like gum on your shoe. You are stuck with it and have trouble getting rid of it. How *can* you get rid of it?

The three main hormones your body produces during fear are epinephrine, norepinephrine, and cortisol. This is referred to as the fight-or-flight response. Epinephrine controls heart rate and metabolism as well as dilating air passages. Norepinephrine speeds up your heart rate, increases blood circulation to your motor muscles, and releases glucose (sugar) from your storage of energy. The increase of blood sugar and metabolism is controlled by cortisol. These bodily chemicals are essential if a charging rhinoceros is gaining on you. But when it occurs due to fear of a future adverse event, whether real or imaginary, your body will still respond with the production of these hormones. Your heart and breathing will race, and your whole being will feel threatened. This causes damaging effects within your body. This is no way to live on a daily basis when thinking of your fear.

Profiles in Dental Courage is the first book of its kind in dealing with and controlling dental fear. As President John F. Kennedy described various Americans and their acts of courage in his original *Profiles in Courage*, this book will tell various stories, in which you will learn how other people have been able to first face, then conquer, their fear of visiting a dental office and so gain all the benefits of modern dentistry. In order to make this information more palatable for you, I have enlisted the aid of entertaining moments laced with compelling and engaging situations. The chapters will alternate between patients' experiences and my four-decade history of creating the perfect system to conquer dental fear for my patients. Using short chapters that conclude with a boxed analysis section, I will help you to understand how you can benefit from the various dental treatments available, without fear and without pain.

I am certain this will prove to be a fun journey into what many feel is an impossible dream. But as the stories unfold, you will discover how thinking outside the box can work miracles for you. These stories consist of hope, optimism, perseverance, determination, and inner success. I will take you on a path of self-examination with the tools necessary to achieve victory in discarding your misconceptions and fear of dentistry.

Along the way you will learn how modern dental treatment is done. Having pioneered the use of one of the lasers in dentistry, I am uniquely qualified to describe the use of ultramodern technologies that will cause you to openly say, "Wow!" Imagine having a computer make your tooth numb painlessly without your lips or tongue being affected. This method is especially ideal for children. My philosophy combines a technologically advanced approach coupled with traditional old-fashioned listening, caring, and explaining. Some call it high tech, high touch. I have also discovered that just by taking the time to explain what the various dental procedures are I can calm my patients down. Their expectation is usually worse than their reality.

I also thought it would be fun and enlightening to intersperse between chapters a *dental tip*.

Through the years I have offered these brief bits of advice to my patients in order for them to keep their teeth for a lifetime. You will find them full of common sense, while other tips are a bit more obscure.

It must be mentioned that I have changed the names of the patients whose stories I tell to honor their privacy. Also, due to convenience, when I refer to the dentist I will write in the generic masculine sense. It will refer to the dentist being male or female.

Though this book may seem autobiographical at times, its intent is to familiarize you with the events that shaped my thinking in order to help others discard their dental phobia.

So, let's have some fun while you learn something new to help yourself or someone you care about.

1

BRADFORD WINSLOW

"Courage is resistance to fear,
mastery of fear—not absence of fear."
—MARK TWAIN

Avoiding eye contact, he looked down at the reception area carpeting with a menacing grimace. Observing him, you would not believe that years ago he was part of an elite covert operations team. He had parachuted from an extraordinary altitude behind enemy lines into North Vietnam. After performing his job, he departed like a phantom in the night awaiting his next assignment. But here he was facing his biggest nightmare: a dental visit. As Bradford Winslow's story unfolds you may find a common point of interest with this most unusual man.

As a captain in the US Marine Corps, he found the need to visit the post dentist on Paris Island. The captain was seated in the treatment chair, and the dentist who entered the operatory was a lieutenant. This recent dental graduate immediately began to inflict pain during a simple dental procedure. The good captain, knowing full well that the specialty grade of the dentist outranked his level of service during dental treatment, accepted the pain without complaining. He, however, secretly vowed never *ever* to return to a dental office again. The pain was too unbearable and upsetting, even for this hard-hitting marine.

It was now fifty-one years later, and the good captain was breaking his vow, sitting in my reception area, because he was experiencing severe dental pain. I walked out to greet him and immediately felt his terror. This proud man wore his feelings like an emblem of fear. His icy-blue eyes turned my blood cold when he picked his head up to look at me. As if I were feeding a deer in the forest, I moved closer to him, very delicately but purposefully. After introductions, I invited him into my conference room, where sixty minutes later, he made an appointment for a pain-free and distracted tooth extraction full of fun and laughter. Winslow's demeanor had completely changed. How could this be? Why must people experience such debilitating fear that it prevents them from enjoying good oral health? How do they acquire these awful feelings? Should the finger of blame be pointed at someone? Is there hope in removing or preventing this fear? To answer these questions we must return to 1970, the beginning of my journey as the dental-phobia miracle man.

2

THE SINGING DENTIST

"Music is the wine that fills the cup of silence."
—ROBERT FRIPP

"But I want to sing and entertain," I said.

"You'll be a dentist, so that I can go to my grave knowing that you'll be able to take care of yourself," my mother answered quite forcefully. With her nonstop harangue, she continued, "Remember, Pat Boone's mother made him get his CPA degree before he entered the music industry. This way if his singing career failed, he'd still have something to fall back on." Rolling my eyes, I knew that there was no way out of this for me. Then she ended her tirade with this common chant: "Besides, you'll be known as the Singing Dentist." It's amazing how her prophesy came to be fulfilled.

I grew up in a family where music was constantly around me. My sister, Arlene, would play the piano while I sang by her side. Most boys idolized famous sports figures. Not so for me. My idol was the world's first great and most famous singing sensation, Al Jolson. No one could wow an audience the way Jolson did. I saw all his films and read everything I could on him. What a personality. He exuded extraordinary raw talent. Confidence and self-esteem poured forth from him with magnetic charm that captivated audiences until the day he died. I sang like him and moved like him. And that's what I wanted to do for the rest of my life. I lived for the feel of being in front of an audience.

Columbia Records noticed me and recorded my demo record. They expressed interest in pursuing a recording contract. I was on my way up the ladder of success.

What a feeling. Then Mom and Dad got wind of this and scuttled my plans. I was still a teenager in college. In fact, I was younger than most since I had skipped the eighth grade. They were adamant about my applying to dental school. New York University College of Dentistry was the only school I applied to. I couldn't have cared less if I had gotten accepted or rejected. But when my letter of acceptance came, I truly fell into an emotional bind. Here was an opportunity to make something of my life as a dentist. Singing might not work out. Realistically, very few people make it to the top. Most perform at weddings, proms, or other local events. Not much of a stable career choice for someone who was contemplating marriage and family. In those days, many of us married young.

"NYU here I come," was my song. More about this career choice later.

So, you might ask, whatever happened to Bradford Winslow?

3

IT'S ALWAYS IN THE STORY

"The human story becomes more and more a
race between education and catastrophe."
—H. G. WELLS

People are funny. I don't mean the ha-ha stuff. We are complicated beings. There are many parts to us. We act in unpredictable ways and are influenced by others in strange ways. Sometimes we act thoughtlessly, producing a severe negative response from another. And many times we are not even aware that our personal behavior produces this reaction.

Let's return to Bradford Winslow.

My heart went out to this man as he accepted my invitation to join me in my unthreatening conference room. The long march to the gallows must have come to his mind as we walked into the room together. Winslow looked puzzled as he sat in the cushioned chair alongside the small cherry wood conference table. This was not what he expected in his meeting with the dentist.

"What are we doing here?" he asked, displaying his disarmed feeling.

"I wanted to speak with you in private," I replied with interest.

"What about?"

"Your story."

"What story?"

"Your wife called me and mentioned something about a bad experience you had with a military dentist. She said you hadn't been to a dentist in fifty-one years," I answered.

He paused to collect his thoughts and said, "What does it matter?"

"It matters a great deal. What's your story? I want to hear it."

Winslow seemed unsure but eventually softened up a bit. He looked away from me and took a few minutes to think. Just before he replied his Adam's apple jumped a little bit from his involuntary swallow. Then he spoke. "That bastard dentist hurt the hell out of me. He kept drilling my tooth without Novocain."

"Why didn't you tell him to stop?"

"In those days you just did what you had to do and didn't question officers, even if they were dentists. It was a God-awful experience."

"What happened when you left the service? Didn't you see a dentist?"

"And have the same painful experience? Not on your life. All you guys are nuts. You go into this profession to hurt people. What's wrong with you guys?"

"What would you prefer?" I said.

I was surprised by his answer. I heard him say, "Why must dental treatment be so painful? I feel so out of control, yet I know I have to do something because my tooth is killing me."

"What if there was a way for you to be in control and not feel a thing?" I offered softly. "Would that interest you?"

"What do you mean?"

"It's exactly as I just said. Nothing to feel and you can control the situation. Look, Bradford, may I call you Bradford?"

"That's my name."

"You are not in the military anymore," I continued. "This is my private dental practice, and I am here to help you in the way you would like to be helped. If I explained to you how I could take care of your dental pain without you feeling it, would that interest you?"

"Yes. But how?"

"What if I had a way of making your teeth numb without your feeling the injection? What if you became so distracted that you didn't really pay attention to treatment? What if you had a fun time?"

"Doc, you sound crazy. How could this be?" He was softening up a bit.

Through logic and simple explanations, Winslow became intrigued and agreed to making an appointment. I did explain that he must leave a deposit for that visit.

"Why are you asking for me to do this?"

"I will follow through on my promise to you. You, on the other hand, must begin to take responsibility for yourself with your teeth. That deposit will be your investment in this visit. It will go toward the treatment I provide. It will also remind you to keep your appointment. That is the only reason it exists. You will not lose it."

After much thought, he agreed.

"My goal is to have you get rid of your fear once and for all, while you pursue good oral health. Medical science has proved that good oral health is essential to good bodily health. I could sedate you, but that would not solve your problem. When you awakened, you would still have your fear."

He smiled at me as he said, "If you make good on all that you've just told me, I'll send lots of people to you."

"Let's make good on that promise. Come with me to the front desk and make your appointment. Oh, by the way, would you mind opening your mouth for me to see the culprit?"

So, he opened his mouth and pointed to the tooth causing him pain. It was rotted down to the gum line and needed removal. "I guess you'll have to remove it. Right?"

"You should have been a dentist, because you're right. It'll be a piece of cake. In the meantime, I'll write you a prescription for medication to ease your pain and prevent infection," I stated. "Would you mind if we took a quick x-ray?"

He agreed.

Winslow kept his appointment and has since become my biggest referrer. All of his dental issues were resolved and transformed into a handsome healthy smile. He keeps all of his preventive visits and has no dental treatment because of this. The patients who maintain their dental hygiene checkup visits rarely experience dental treatment.

ANALYSIS

Tell me a story

We all have a story to tell. In the case of fear there is always a story to share with others. When the patient visits the dentist, that moment should be exclusively for the patient, not the dentist, and not the staff. The patient is the star, front and center stage. And he has a story to tell. The dentist must get the patient to tell it. At some time, somewhere, the patient underwent a negative dental experience that produced a fearful memory that has prevented further dental treatment. The patient needs to tell his story. Just as important, the dentist must listen. It must be a sincere, sympathetic, compassionate, engaged type of listening. Bradford Winslow's act of telling his story must have been a liberating moment. Finally, somebody was listening nonjudgmentally. He was no longer alone in his thoughts. Just the simple act of listening can sometimes be enough to create the breakthrough needed to help the patient succeed in destroying his fear. It sounds simple enough, yet most dentists do not take the time to perform this most basic human process. We all want to be heard.

DENTAL TIP:

Baby Bottle Tooth Syndrome

Never, never, never give your child a bottle of milk or juice before going to sleep and then leave it there unattended overnight. If you must place a bottle in the child's mouth, fill it with water instead.

Carbohydrate-rich liquids in the mouth overnight are a recipe for severe tooth decay. This photograph demonstrates the dentally fatal consequences in ignoring this advice.

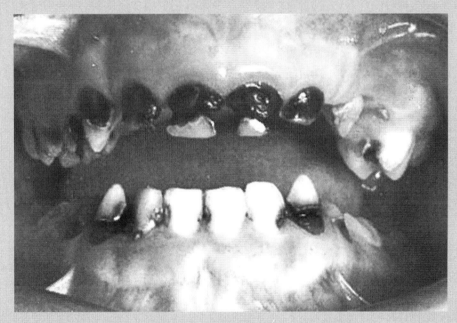

Caption: Do not let this be your child.

4

SWEET DREAMS AND PLEASANT FEELINGS

"A man without ambition is dead."
—PEARL BAILEY

"Do you ever extract teeth?" I asked the dentist.

"Of course," he replied, rather confused by the question.

"Do you ever place a denture in the mouth right after that extraction?" I continued.

"Sometimes."

"Would you place denture adhesive on that denture to prevent it from falling out?"

"Sometimes."

"Wouldn't the denture hurt the patient at that extraction site when they bit down?"

"Yes, it could."

"What if I could show you a new denture adhesive cream that would not only hold the denture in place, but it would make the patient numb at the extraction site for better comfort? Would that interest you?" I finally asked.

"Yes, I'm interested. Please go on."

During my freshman year at New York University College of Dentistry I received a grant in the form of a summer position for a drug company. They had me travel to many dentists in Queens, New York City, to explain and demonstrate their latest products. This was a great learning experience for me. One day I visited the oral surgery practice of Dr. Bertram Blum. His partner, Dr. David Schwartz was there. We spoke about the company's products. He turned out to be a better salesman than me. He sold me on the wonders of oral surgery and invited me to return on a routine basis to learn it through assisting him and his partner after school hours and on weekends. I took the bait and became hooked on the clinical aspects of my new profession.

That summer I made my quota of daily rounds in the mornings and spent the afternoons with him. There is a lot to be said for apprenticing. One of the procedures he performed was intravenous sedation. This is a process by which a needle was placed in the patient's vein, and a mild sedative was injected. These surgeons would always say to the patient, just before the patient was about to go under, "Sweet dreams and pleasant feelings." The patient then became briefly drowsy. The more significant feature is that it produced amnesia while the dental procedure was being done. The patient was then made numb, had the surgery completed, woke up, and did not remember a thing. The first time I witnessed this I was amazed at how cool it was.

That first summer I started to see patterns in some of these procedures. I noticed the fearful patients with their white knuckles grabbing the armrest. I observed patients not listening to most of what the doctors were telling them. Their fear was so overwhelming that it prevented them from being more engaged in their treatment. They just wanted it over with and to depart from the office. But, it was that awful fear that covered them like a death shroud.

Throughout my three years with Blum and Schwartz their extensive resources were made available to me. They enrolled me in a summer externship at Long Island Jewish Hospital Department of Dentistry. As time progressed, I realized that I enjoyed much more than oral surgery and wanted to pursue a general practice concept. Specialization would have limited my interests. There was one common thread, however, that coursed through all the areas of dentistry. It was fear. Fear knows no boundaries. That's when I knew that I wanted to help people with dental fear as part of my general practice. Besides, I loved challenges and thinking outside of the box.

Having graduated from New York University College of Dentistry, I continued my postgraduate education in a general practice residency program at Jamaica Hospital in Jamaica, Queens, New York.

This provided me with the experience of a lifetime. I helped some of the survivors from a major plane crash at JFK Airport. Now what does a dentist have to do with a plane crash? More about this later. Let's get back to eradicating fear in the world of dentistry.

DENTAL TIP:

Only floss those you want to keep!

Brush your teeth twice a day with fluoride toothpaste. Floss your teeth twice a day. Bacteria always live in our mouths. They are living, moving beings constantly on the search for nutritional sustenance. Food that you leave behind between your teeth is a smorgasbord for them. What do all living things do after they eat? They go to the bathroom. They eliminate waste. Bacterial waste is acidic. The bacteria know to return to the areas in your mouth where food clings. After repeated bacterial visits to your tooth their acid droppings begin to rob your tooth of its minerals within the enamel. That is how decay or a cavity begins to form. This is the beginning of needless dental treatment that could have been easily prevented just by flossing and brushing routinely. Adhering to this advice will be well worth your time in reading this book. An ounce of prevention is certainly worth a pound of cure.

5

"AND THY STAFF THEY COMFORT ME"

Yea, though I walk through the valley of the shadow of
death, I will fear no evil: for thou art with me; thy rod and
thy staff they comfort me.
—PSALMS 23:4 KING JAMES VERSION 1611

See this image in your mind's eye. Doctor's sparse cold waiting room. Out-of-date magazines scattered on tabletops. Glass window partition separating waiting room from gum-chewing, telephone-gossiping receptionist. Entering this office you are not greeted. In fact, you are almost ignored. Her finger might point to a sign-in sheet for you to initial. Then the interminable waiting begins. You haven't seen the doctor, and yet your gut tells you that this whole scene is somehow wrong. Your stomach never lies. Your problem is that you don't pay attention to the message it's sending you. To better understand this, let's get back to the Bible.

It's highly doubtful that when King David of ancient Israel wrote these lines he was referring to dentistry. We can rest easy that he was alluding to the comfort of the Good Lord. But, if we look deeper into those lines there is a word that can help the fearful dental patient. It is *staff*. David had it right when he wrote that *thy* staff *they comfort me.*

The doctor's staff is the most significant part of his office. Yes, the staff should comfort the patient. You should feel welcomed. You should not be an intrusion on their day but the reason for their day. If the purpose of life is a life full of purpose, then you should be the purpose of their day.

Now, picture this image instead. Elevator door opens onto the second floor. Soft music washes over you as you enter the cherry wood-lined reception area. Cushioned carpeting comforts your path as you walk to the unobstructed wood and marble front desk. A greeter stands and says your name in the form of a sincerely welcoming greeting. No glass partition exists to segregate you from the staff. As in the hit TV show *Cheers*, everybody knows your name. After being received warmly, you spot the beverage center and make yourself a fresh cup of coffee. Just before sitting with your drink, you grab a copy of the latest magazine while you relax in a comfortable chair gazing at the fireplace. One word comes to mind in this room, calm. There is a celebration of calm and recognition in this space.

Which image would you prefer? Let's see what Allison Kruger had to say about all of this.

As Meena lifted the telephone to her ear, even before she could announce the name of our office, she was surprised by the sound of sobbing from the other end of the line. Having been put off guard, she asked, "How may I serve you?" in a mildly perplexed manner.

The caller was in tears. With mournful sniffles, she said, "I am so scared. I am so scared."

"Scared of what?" Meena asked.

In a staccato fashion the caller continued, "I am so frightened of the dentist. My front crown just fell out of my mouth. I can't walk around like this. I know he'll hurt me. I am so afraid of the dentist."

"I'm Meena. What's your name?"

Sobbing, she replied, "I'm Allison Kruger. Can Dr. Passes help me? I'm so scared."

"Absolutely. You're going to love him. All the patients love the way he listens. In fact, all of our doctors and staff feel the same way. They genuinely care and take their time with you. And Dr. Passes will definitely not hurt you."

"Are you sure? I'm so scared."

"I am sure. So many people, just like you, have conquered their dental fear. Why don't I arrange for a free consultation so that you'll be able to meet him and discuss your concerns?"

And so the telephone conversation went on with Meena reassuring Allison that she will be doing the right thing for herself. They spoke for a total of twenty minutes, not the usual three minutes, until Allison made her appointment.

The morning of Allison's visit, during our daily staff huddle, Meena filled the staff in on her conversation with Allison to ensure that we as a *team* would be ready for her. Everyone wanted to make sure that she would have a very special appointment with us. Her concern became everyone's concern.

When I first saw Allison, she was sitting in my reception area, crying her eyes out. Meena and my insurance administrator went to calm her down with words of reassurance, telling her softly that everything would be fine. Lavanda, my clinical assistant, appeared in the reception area ready to escort Allison to the treatment room. As she introduced Lavanda to Allison, Meena briefly explained how Allison was feeling. With a reassuring smile Lavanda put her hand on Allison's shoulder and offered words and actions of comfort and encouragement. When we finally spoke in my treatment room, Allison's first words to me were, "You have the most wonderful staff. Meena and now Lavanda have been so kind to me. They seem to truly understand my feelings. I work in a doctor's office, and believe me, the staff there does not treat the patients in the same manner. You are very fortunate to have them."

"Thank you, Allison. That's very kind of you to say these words. My entire staff is trained to treat our patients with care, compassion, comfort, and consideration. Frankly, it's rather simple; we treat people in the same manner that we would like to be treated."

Seeing her deluge of tears discontinue, I decided to turn my attention to her area of concern. "So, please tell me your story. What has made you feel this way?"

Without missing a beat, she answered, "When I was younger, I was hurt. My mother took me to this dentist who pulled some of my baby teeth out without numbing me. It was horrible. I can still remember the visit like it was yesterday. I can't get it out of my mind."

Some tears started to well up in her eyes. I reached out to her shoulder and comforted her as I spoke. "What if I told you that it doesn't have to be that way?"

"But the dentists I have seen just keep working, even if I complain that it's hurting."

"Things are not like that here. We think about and treat people differently. Just take a look at our conversation we are having now. How many times have you spoken with a dentist as we are doing right now?"

"Never. But how will you not hurt me with the needle?" Her tears stopped, and I knew we were beginning to make progress. That's when I told her how we would do it. There are many options I have in providing pain-free dentistry. In the following chapters I will go into greater detail on how this is accomplished.

After a thirty-minute conversation Allison decided to make an appointment to fix her tooth. When we were finished, she was so surprised and satisfied that she told the world on her Facebook page. We have since received more referrals from her. When she left, she turned to me and said, "Thank you, Dr. Passes. I know that you can help me." Then she ended her comments with, "I am sick and tired of being a *dental cripple*!"

Wow! Talk about coining a phrase.

Analysis

Staff, Staff, Staff

I can't begin to overemphasize the importance of properly trained staff. It is essential that the doctor's staff represents him in the most caring and professional manner possible. There is no excuse for ignoring this rule. This, however, does not occur by accident. Every day, my staff and I undergo training and reinforcement on what the appropriate ideals and behavior should be for our staff. We never forget who the star is. It is you, the patient. We always remember that our purpose is to help the patient in the most comfortable and effectively reassuring pain-free manner. We must always take into consideration the patient's feelings.

When a patient becomes emotionally difficult, we do not roll our eyes and act rude. Rather, we take the time to understand what caused the patient to feel that way. Communication is also important. How can we help you if we are not on the same page? Staff must be engaged with you, the patient. All of this is plain old common sense.

DENTAL TIP:

How frequently should you get a cleaning?

Periodontal studies have shown that bacteria will always live in your mouth. All that we can do is to minimize the numbers of their population. After much research it has been shown that after you get a cleaning it takes about ninety days for bacteria to regroup and rebuild their population within your mouth. That is three months. If you wait another three months, then not only will their numbers be much higher but they will now have the ability to bring on greater acid destruction of your teeth, bone, and gums.

Insurance companies only pay for cleanings every six months. It is important for you to realize that this is the longest you should wait for a cleaning.

Remember, gums should not bleed when you brush your teeth. Bleeding is a sign of dental disease and needs to be treated. How would you feel if your hands bled every time you washed them?

Now you know the rest of the story.

6

"BE PATIENT.
YOUR TIME WILL COME."

*"A handful of patience is worth more than
a bushel of brains"*
—DUTCH PROVERB

I n 1974 I graduated from New York University College of Dentistry. How proud my parents were. I was on my way to becoming the Singing Dentist. But first I had to do a general practice residency in a hospital. During my dental school years, I was fortunate to meet many dentists who invited me to observe their clinical procedures. This three-year externship complemented my education at NYU. It was to be my privilege to meet Paul Kaufman, an oral surgeon in Queens, New York. Kaufman was not only an accomplished surgeon but he was also the chairman of the Department of Dentistry at Jamaica Hospital. I spent three years with him. He suggested that I visit Lewis Gilmore, a superb general dentist in Jamaica, Queens, and the director of the hospital's emerging dental residency program. It was made clear, due to budgetary constraints, that there would be only one resident that first year. The competition would be fierce for that one position. When the time came for me to apply to their program they had already been observing me for three years.

The night after my interview I received a phone call from Dr. Gilmore. "Harvey, if you want the residency position, it's yours."

Thrilled beyond words, I replied, "Absolutely. Thank you so much. I can't tell you how happy I am."

"It's not that simple. You'll be getting a call from Dr. Kaufman. He wants to meet with you to discuss something else with you."

"Does it affect my acceptance?"

"Maybe, but probably not, knowing you. He'll call you in the morning."

I spent the whole night trying to figure out what Dr. Kaufman wanted to discuss with me. When the alarm went off, I had finally just fallen asleep. What a lousy way to greet the new day. Later that day I got the anxiously anticipated phone call from Dr. Kaufman.

"Congratulations, Harvey."

"Thank you, Dr. Kaufman. Dr. Gilmore said that there was something you wanted to discuss with me."

"Yes, there is. I'd like to meet with you to discuss it. Can you meet for lunch this Saturday?"

Apprehensively, I answered, "Sure. What's this all about?"

"Don't worry. Everything is fine. I just need to go over some things with you."

"Okay." Then we made the date as my anxiety began to subside.

Saturday came. We met at a local diner. As we sat down in the booth, Dr. Kaufman extended his hand in a congratulatory fashion. Then he said, "Do you know why we picked you above all of the other candidates?"

"No."

"I'll tell you a story to make my point clear to you. When Dr. Gilmore and I started this department years ago, we had the dream of creating a teaching division. Sure, we and many other dentists have been here providing dental care to indigent people. But, there were no residents to teach. Finally, after much politicking, we raised enough money to begin our program."

Unsure of where this was leading, I remained silent until he got to the point. I certainly did not want to interrupt his story.

"All of the other departments in the hospital," he continued, "were skeptical about our new program. Some said that it was a waste of money and resources. I knew that we needed a special individual who would understand the politics behind this residency." He picked up his coffee cup and composed his thoughts for what he was about to say to me.

"As our first resident, you will set the precedent for all who follow. What will make your job challenging is the fact that not only will you be on call for twenty-four hours a day for twelve days, with two days off every two weeks, but there is something more."

Here it comes. What more could he expect?

"You will have to become our ambassador to the rest of the hospital."

What was he talking about? I didn't get it at first, but then it dawned on me what this was all about.

"We have gotten to know you for the past three years. You will make a very good dentist, but you also have the capacity to listen and understand people. Various doctors in the hospital will not know what to do with you. They have never worked with a dentist before. They will laugh at you and try to knock down your ego. We believe you to be strong enough to take it and bide your time. We know that you will do the right thing and keep your mouth shut while swallowing your pride until the right time comes to prove yourself."

Finally understanding his concerns, I felt more at ease once I knew what I was up against. "So how do you want me to conduct myself?"

"That's why we accepted you. You're already doing the right thing with your question. You've got the idea. Just use your instincts and know when to keep quiet and when to speak. See the big picture. I promise you it will be worth it. Be patient. *Your time will come.*"

DENTAL TIP:

Chewing gum is good for you?

After twenty years of research, Wrigley discovered that chewing sugar-free gum three times a day for twenty minutes each will diminish decay. The American Dental Association agreed with this finding. Here's how this works. Every time you chew food you lose the minerals within your enamel. Your body's natural healing mechanism uses your saliva to replace the tooth's lost minerals. If you chew with sugar-free gum, salivary production will be stimulated, washing over the enamel with mineral-rich saliva. This will help to rebuild your tooth. To be brutally honest, you could get the same results by chewing on a rubber band. It does not have to be Wrigley gum. Get any sugar-free gum and keep it in your pocket as an after-meal dental treat to help you ward off Mr. Tooth Decay. Or chew on a rubber band!

7

IT WAS WORTH WAITING FOR.

"If it is worth waiting for, then it was worth
waiting for. Perseverance."
—ANONYMOUS

And so it went. During the first month of my training, I found myself in the operating room learning general anesthesia. Most of the medical interns chose to skip this training. They were not going to become anesthesiologists and saw no relevance. I, however, found this to be exciting, since I already understood the use of sedation in dentistry from the oral surgeons. What a learning experience it was. Technically, it taught me all of the fundamental principles necessary to administer anesthesia. Similarly, on a personal level, it offered me the most profound growth in self-esteem and self-confidence. Imagine what it takes to be in a situation where someone's life is in your hands. You are responsible for rendering unconsciousness and then waking them.

When one is under general anesthesia it is imperative that an open airway be maintained. There is a procedure called endotracheal intubation. This involves placing a plastic tube in one's throat and administering medical gasses as well as oxygen to the patient. The technique is somewhat different today than it was in 1974. Endotracheal intubation is a skillful procedure. If placed wrong in those days, the tube could wind up in the stomach, and the patient would be denied oxygen, causing a respiratory and cardiac emergency potentially resulting in death.

During my first month in the anesthesia rotation, I was taught how to perform this technique. Frankly, I became quite skilled at it. To reward my intense desire to excel in this, the chairman of the Department of Anesthesia allowed me to become part of the cardiac arrest team. This meant that when the public address system blurted out, "Code 99, code 99, room 324, room 324," I had to run to that room to participate in the cardiopulmonary resuscitation of a cardiac-arrested patient. I was about to realize Dr. Kaufman's prophesy. He had said, "Just use your instincts and know when to keep quiet and when to speak. See the big picture. I promise you it will be worth it. Be patient. *Your time will come.*"

Scene: I enter room 324. Patient is on the floor after having gotten out of bed and fallen after his heart decided to quit. Doctors surround the patient. Cardiac arrest medical emergency cart is open, with all of its paraphernalia spread all over. Doctor is leaning over patient trying to intubate him.

I think, "That doctor has no idea how to intubate that patient. Should I say something?"

Scene: Chief medical resident notices me and rudely, arrogantly, and cruelly says out loud to everyone attending the dying patient, "Oh, look. It's the dental resident." Then to me, "I don't think we need to check his teeth right now. If he makes it, we'll call you to give him a cleaning." Laughter was heard while that poor soul of a patient unconsciously waited to be resuscitated.

At that moment I fully understood all that Dr. Kaufman had said to me. This was it. Now I was expected to shut my mouth and just take it. It reminded me of what Branch Rickey, the general manager of the Brooklyn Dodgers, said on August 28, 1945, to the first black major league baseball player, Jackie Robinson, before being signed with the team. "Shut your mouth, and take all of the grief you'll be getting. Your time will come. Can you wait it out?"

To Dr. Kaufman, I had said, "Yes, I will wait it out." I had absolutely no idea what I was in for. Now, I did. So, I shut my mouth and left the room only to hear chuckles from the other doctors behind my back as they bungled their life saving measures to the patient's detriment. Incredibly, they did not muffle their sarcastic jocularity. And so it went for the next week. I would respond to the Code 99 alert but stand around and do nothing while I was viewed with ridicule. Then, it happened, my redemption.

One morning I attended a little girl who had fallen off her bicycle and split her upper lip. Finishing her suturing I heard the tinny harsh blare from the public address system, "Code 99, emergency room. Code 99, emergency room." I was in one of the treatment suites in the ER. I stepped into the hallway and asked where the Code had been called. A nurse pointed to another room. Walking in I saw the same chief medical resident trying to intubate the patient. Frankly, he still didn't look like he knew what he was doing. Not wanting to be humiliated again, I just walked out, back to my patient in the other room. As a nurse was speaking to the little girl's mother, giving her postoperative instructions, another medical resident ran in asking, "Does anyone know how to intubate?"

"I do," I proudly replied.

"Quick, get in the other room and help us."

Within a minute I had intubated the patient while the chief medical resident watched in wonder. Successfully completing my task, I went back into the other room again to finish writing my chart on the little girl referred to as the "bicycle lip" patient. A few minutes later the chief medical resident came in looking for me. Grabbing my hand and shaking it, he said, "I owe you an apology. I treated you poorly. You didn't deserve it. If not for you, that patient in the other room might have died. Your skill saved him. I had no idea that you were that good at intubation. Would you accept my apology?"

Remembering Dr. Kaufman's words, I just said, "Sure. I appreciate what you just said."

"Can we call upon you whenever we have a code to intubate the patient?"

"Absolutely."

Now I understood how Jackie Robinson felt after proving himself in major league baseball. It felt good, really good. I called Dr. Kaufman and sensed his smile of approval across the telephone line after I recounted my experience to him. He said, "And that's one of the reasons why we picked you. I knew you could do it. Now things will be easier for you. Good luck. I'm proud of you. From this point on, the rest of the hospital will look at our department differently."

Nothing beats recognition. It's a great confidence builder. It was worth waiting for.

DENTAL TIP:

Eat cheese for a healthy smile

I'll bet you didn't know that having your child eat cheese can prevent cavities. New research shows that by snacking on Swiss, Monterey Jack, mozzarella and cheddar cheese, high quantities of calcium will be absorbed into your child's teeth thereby increasing its protection against decay. These cheeses also promote your child's salivary glands to wash away food debris while protecting their teeth from the acids that weaken them. The calcium and phosphorous also helps to remineralize the enamel. Now you know why the photographer always says, "Say cheese!"

8

STOP NEEDLING ME

*"Inventions reached their limit long ago, and I see no hope
for further development."*
—JULIUS FRONTINUS, FIRST CENTURY AD

*"As everything that can be invented has been invented, I see
no need to keep the patent office open."*
—THOMAS JEFFERSON

"No offense, doc, but I hate dentists."

"Me, too, but what's your reason?" I replied, thinking I had made a joke.

"It's those damn needles. They hurt, and I can't speak or eat properly for at least an hour. My tongue and lips become so numb that they feel useless. I own and operate a diner and need to speak to people without feeling and looking like I had a stroke."

"What if there was a way for you to become numb and not feel it? Would that make things better for you?"

"Sure, but how is that possible? And what about my not being able to eat or speak for a long time?"

"That could also be managed in most cases," I replied.

One thing that has made American dentistry the envy of the world for over a hundred years is our dental manufacturers. Old challenges are being conquered with new technical solutions every day. After all, this is a big concern for most patients with much money to be made by these manufacturers. So, allow me to tell you a story about painless injections for the majority of us. It occurred almost two decades ago.

After developing the clinical applications for the Holmium: YAG laser in dentistry and becoming a founding member of the Academy of Laser Dentistry, I became well known in my profession. A company created a dental machine called the Single Tooth Anesthesia Device. They contacted me to try this new way to give an injection. They stated that it incorporated a small computer to help deliver local anesthetic to the individual tooth with the patient rarely feeling it and without the collateral numbness to the lips or tongue. Intrigued, I tried it and after a small learning curve found it to be as claimed by the company. My greatest feeling of accomplishment is when I have a parent witness their child becoming numb for a filling without any indication of pain. (Did you know that parents always have their children undergo treatment first, in a new dental office, before they make an appointment for themselves?)

The company was so pleased to have my endorsement that they asked me to address their annual stockholder's meeting at the American Stock Exchange on my experiences with it. The press happened to be there and wrote an article on it. *CBS News* saw the article and interviewed me on their nightly news show.

Then we got the phone call from John Zemekis, an average every day individual with an extraordinary amount of dental fear. "I'm leaving for Europe in two days but have a terrible toothache. I have not been to the dentist in twenty years. I am deathly afraid of the needle. I just saw Dr. Passes on *CBS News* describing a new type of pain-free injection. Does it really work?"

"Absolutely. You'll love it. If it works great on children, it will be perfect for you," stated my receptionist.

So, John made an appointment. When he came in, we spent much time describing how this most beneficial technology works. He was impressed and allowed me to use it while restoring his tooth without pain. He could not believe how easy it all was. When he left, he stated that if everything was that simple he would return for a full checkup after he came back from Europe. We took bets to see if he'd return. To my surprise, he did. We became good friends. His family and friends were referred to my office.

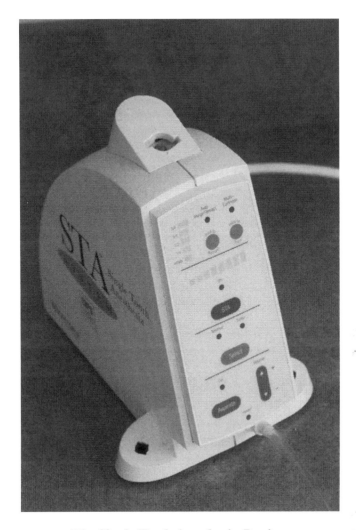

The Single Tooth Anesthesia Device

ANALYSIS

Sometimes all it takes is listening, caring and explaining. John asked a simple question regarding how the equipment works. During this explanation we built up rapport. He felt comfortable with the answer and decided to try it. We followed through on our promise to him. I ascribe to the rule that **BLT** = **R**. *The patient must first* **B***elieve you. Then they* **L***ike you. Finally they* **T***rust you. All of this equals* **R***espect. It's all rather simple.*

HERE'S HOW STA WORKS.

The problem

Years ago a colleague of mine pondered the question on how to give an injection without getting the other structures numb. The challenge lay in the fact that the upper and lower jaws are different. The upper jaw is made up of porous bone. This means that the administration of local anesthetic can be accomplished by simply placing the tip of the needle in the approximate site of the tip of the root. Picture an upside down ice cream cone. That's what the root might look like within the upper jaw. At the tip of the root the nerve travels through and into the tooth providing the tooth sensation. By blocking the nerve pathway at that site you become numb. So will your lip and cheek. The lower jaw is much different. It does not have porous bone. This bone is more like concrete. One cannot inject there at the tip of the root to get you numb. The bone is so dense that the local anesthetic will not pass through. The way to get you numb is to find the main nerve trunk in the back of either side of your jaw. Upon injecting that site, the side of your jaw will become numb. This includes the same side of your tongue, lips, teeth and gums. And, those block injections can last from one to three hours making speech compromised.

The solution

It was discovered that if you place local anesthetic alongside the root of the tooth it could travel down its length until reaching the root's tip. The anesthetic could then make just that tooth numb. The tongue, lip and gums would not be effected by it. Here's the challenge; how can you get the local anesthetic down this very narrow pathway to the root's tip? Hand pressure from a traditional dental syringe is not strong enough to accomplish this. The solution was nothing short of genius.

A digital solution

An extremely thin narrow needle was developed and attached through a clear plastic tube to a small box containing a computer chip. A foot pedal was then added for the doctor to control this dental device. The thin hair-like needle is placed painlessly within the small space between the gum and the root. The doctor's foot engages the pedal and local anesthetic begins to flow down the side of the root to the tip. Here's where the genius lies. The digital chip records the amount of backpressure that space is producing. In less than a blink of your eye it calculates how much pressure the pump should produce to get the anesthetic down without causing you pain. Your hand cannot do this. This injection takes longer to give but it overcomes all of your most common objections. Patients don't even know their numb except for the absence of pain. People who speak for a living, such as teachers, sales people etc. love this new solution to an old problem. Also works great on children.

DENTAL TIP:

Teething Pain

Parents should wipe their newborn's gums with a clean, damp cloth or soft moist gauze after each feeding to control the accumulation of plaque and to establish this ritual as part of baby's daily routine.

What most people are unaware of is that formula or breast milk contains high amounts of carbohydrates, which bacteria feed on. If this milk is left on the gum pads, inflammation and gum irritation will occur during your baby's dental eruption of teeth. Amazing as it sounds, just by wiping clean this excess milk, it will cut down on teething pains.

Another interesting fact is that this preventive act will initiate good habits in your child, thus keeping his teeth clean for the rest of his life.

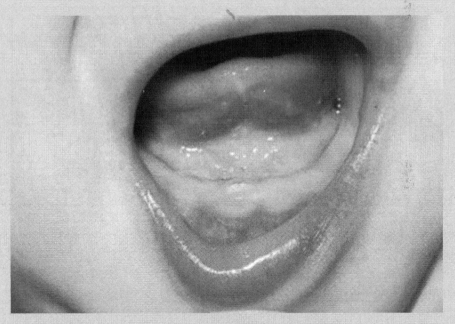

Baby's teeth are growing under those cute little gums.

9

FROGGY

"Hard work's a good distraction."
—SCOTT WESTERFELD

"Now, what kind of a ridiculous chapter title is that?" you may ask yourself. Frankly, it's ingenious. The simplest things make the greatest impact on people. Most people do not have a severe fear of the dentist. They do, however, have trouble with not being in control while in the dental chair. Check out this next story to learn the power of our cute little green amphibian.

Herb Klausner is a new patient who is a retired economics professor. With specific ideas on what he wants, Herb states that he requires his dentistry to be performed in a certain fashion, especially without X-rays. He is not particularly afraid of the dentist but does have the need to be in control of the situation. Lying on his back with his mouth open while the dentist uses metallic mechanized instruments in his oral stoma produces a feeling of intense vulnerability in him.

"There's something about lying here helpless with my mouth open that disturbs me," Herb said, hoping to evoke a laugh.

"Would you be surprised if I told you that I've heard that complaint countless times?"

"I guess not, but that still doesn't address my concern. Isn't there something that you can do to alleviate this?'

Knowing that what I am about to do would provoke a response of absurd credulity from Herb, I asked, "Would you like to meet Froggy?"

With a popeyed expression, eyebrows touching the ceiling, and a look of perplexed disbelief, this all-too-serious gentleman who had lectured students for years on the intricacies of our financial system answered, "Who the hell is Froggy?"

A smile spread across my face as I spun around in my dental stool to open a drawer and take out Froggy. I handed Froggy to Herb while I formally introduced them to each other. "Herb, meet Froggy. Froggy, say hello to Herb."

Froggy

Herb looked at me as if he thought I had totally lost my mind. He just stared for what must have felt like a very long second at Froggy and asked, "What is this?"

"Froggy is our patients' patron saint. When you feel the need to be in control of your dental visit, you just turn Froggy over and squeeze his rump with your thumb. You see, it's just an old-fashioned snapper that we used to use as a child. That snapping noise is loud, and I will hear it. When I do hear it, I'll immediately stop what I am doing, allowing you to wrest control over your treatment."

Intensely scrutinizing Froggy, Herb began to smile. Then he laughed as the simplistic brilliance of this concept dawned on him. "You're amazing. This is a wonderful idea. My biggest problem was not being in control. This is great. I like the way you think."

Then Herb had fun trying out his new toy as Froggy's snapping sound was heard over and over again.

"Shall we begin?" I asked.

Laughing out loud Herb responded, "Absolutely." And, so it went. Only once did Herb squeeze Froggy, as a test to see if I would truly stop. Almost everyone does that. After that, he never did it again. He did, however, steal Froggy in order to perform a "show and tell" with everyone he knew about this simple strategy. Can you imagine being referred to a dental office because of Froggy? And, yes, it happens.

By the way Herb returned Froggy.

ANALYSIS

Building Rapport

As I mentioned earlier, everyone has a story to tell. The trick is to get them to tell it. In Herb's case it was control. Sometimes the very idea of having some power over the dental visit is all that is necessary for the patient to feel comfortable. Just knowing that we will stop treatment when the patient indicates that need is all that is required. An unsophisticated, almost child-like instrument, Froggy, is the only requisite to get the job done and even build rapport. Little things can produce large effects.

DENTAL TIP

"People with dentures should not eat artificial sweeteners. It will cause artificial cavities."
Mitch Hedberg

10

THE CRASH OF EASTERN FLIGHT 66

"There is no discipline in the world so severe as the discipline
of experience subjected to the tests of intelligent development
and direction."
—JOHN DEWEY

"We'll monitor this patient's progress as his bones begin to heal in his cheek," Dr. Kaufman said to me as we went back to the clinic after our surgical procedure in the operating room at Jamaica Hospital. With a thunderous boom, the storm outside was gaining intensity as the wind began to howl. We were on our way to the clinic conference room, where he was going to lecture to me and my new junior dental resident on oral surgery. All of a sudden the public address system blurted out, "Attention, all personnel. Code blue. I repeat—code blue. This is not a drill. Code blue." We just looked at each other. What the heck was code blue?

I picked up the hospital phone and asked the operator that same question. Her reply stunned me. "Code blue," she said, "is a major catastrophe where all patients not in critical care need to be removed from the hospital due to an influx of a large number of casualties from a major disaster."

"What happened?"

"Eastern Airlines flight 66 just crashed on landing at JFK Airport during this horrific storm. The survivors, if there are any, are being brought to us."

The three of us went down to the emergency room to see what was going on and how we could help. Somehow we got separated. Then, the most ridiculous event happened, which to this day I still chuckle about. I found myself with the chairman of the Department of Surgery, a man who should have retired long ago but just couldn't give up his authority. "You," pointing to me. "Come over here."

"Yes, Dr. Ballantine."

"Aren't you the dental resident?"

"Yes, Dr. Ballantine."

"Hmm. Let me see. Yes, go to the survivors and check for gingivitis."

I was just getting used to being stunned that day, but this was absolutely ludicrous. "You want me to check to see who has gum disease after they've been in a major plane crash? Is that right?" Disbelief melted on my face as I saw him nod. I just replied that I was on my way to do so as I shook my head from side to side.

Leaving this mad hatter behind, I searched for Dr. Kaufman. Upon finding him, I recounted my moment in the theater of the absurd. He laughed out loud and said, "That's Dr. Ballantine. Let's forget him and see what we can do. Check for gum disease! What a stupid order to give. With people struggling for their lives, why would we check for gum disease?"

The hospital was being treated as if this were an episode on the popular TV show *MASH*. The large auditorium had all the chairs moved to one side. Victims were brought in on stretchers. I remember going to one gentleman who was unconscious and burnt all over. A surgeon came over and asked me to intubate him, keeping his airway open while connecting him to oxygen. During this time he was addressing the survivor's wounds. After that I joined Dr. Kaufman with another lucky survivor.

We started burn treatment. Somehow there were not enough doctors to handle this flood of victims. We remained there for about eight hours until things started to level out with all the right care needed. That day, June 24, 1975, of the 124 people on board, 106 passengers and six crew members died. Ten passengers and ten flight attendants, who were seated in the rear of the aircraft, survived. One surviving passenger died nine days later from injuries sustained in the accident.

That night was to be my graduation dinner from the general practice residency program. All of my attendings were waiting for Dr. Kaufman and me to join them at a restaurant for a farewell dinner. It was to be an evening full of good camaraderie, admiration, and fun. These doctors had been wonderful to me, and I loved and respected them all.

"I don't know how you managed to do this. This was certainly the best test to see how I would handle myself during an emergency. You didn't have to go that far for me to demonstrate my abilities." They all laughed as they raised a glass to toast me. Then I was asked to give a short speech on my opinion of the program.

"I learned how to do root canal treatment, crown and bridge, fillings, extract teeth, perform in the operating room, and so much more. But there is one intangible skill that this program provided me, for which I will be forever grateful:

confidence and self-esteem. Today's shocking experience brought me face-to-face with how I will conduct myself during a severe emergency. I have a different appreciation and perspective on things. What might normally have caused me anxiety seems less relevant than more significant circumstances. Routine dental treatment is easier to handle now."

There was somber silence as everyone thought about the day's events.

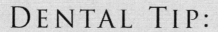 # DENTAL TIP:

Your Child's First Visit

Believe it or not, you should take your child to the dentist no later than six months after the first tooth erupts or at least sometime before the first birthday.

Natural dental anxiety can be diminished if you take your young child with you to your routine dental visit. This allows your child to become accustomed to the sights, sounds, and smells of the dental office. It will also give the dentist and staff an opportunity to meet with your child and establish a positive connection early in life.

The more your child recognizes the staff and becomes familiar with them the smaller the chance of him feeling threatened by them.

11

THE ABSOLUTE BEST
NUMBING CREAM

*"If you are distressed by anything external, the pain is not
due to the thing itself, but to your estimate of it; and this you
have the power to revoke at any moment."*
—MARCUS AURELIUS ANTONINUS (121–180 AD)

"I must tell you, I never feel your injections. How do you do it?" asked David Raskoff. "I'm not fearful, but you make this extremely easy."

So many times a day I hear those words from my patients. It's especially gratifying to hear them from my phobic patients in a tone of great disbelief and amazement. My favorite and most common comment I hear before the injection is given, "Doc, I'm the worst patient you'll ever have. No one is worse than me. Trust me, no one."

"Trust me," I say, "you're not the worst. But everyone feels they are."

When I first began my career in private practice, I purchased a numbing gel from my dental supplier. It was mostly 20 percent benzocaine in a gooey gel with a syrupy flavor. I placed this on the gum and waited five minutes for the numbing effect to occur. I gave the injection, and the patient said, "Ouch, you're hurting me!" This was not a very good way to begin one's career.

After a few years, I began to think how I might be able to improve on this challenge. After much research and trial and error, I came up with a formula that I had compounded for me in a pharmacy. This cream is incredibly effective, especially with my new technique in administering an injection, and it is a rarity for a patient to feel anything at all during the injection of local anesthesia. Due to proprietary reasons, I cannot disclose what is in it.

ANALYSIS

Follow through

"Say what you mean and mean what you say." I cannot overstate the importance of following through with a promise made to the patients. In order for patients to believe you, like you, and trust you, the dentist cannot hurt them, if you say that you will not. The use of the most advanced technology and techniques should be incorporated to follow through on this promise. Though nothing in this world is 100 percent, if patients should feel anything, then we choose a different technique to help them. We never give up. There should be numerous tricks in our bag of therapies.

Once patients have a comfortable experience, they begin to bring down some of their walls of fear. It's all a matter of trust, follow-through and making good on the promise.

DENTAL TIP:

How to find the right dentist for you

You have moved into a new neighborhood or your dentist has moved out of yours. You need a dentist but are not sure how to go about doing this. Indeed, how do you find a dentist? And, how do you find the right one? What follows is a bulleted list on how to achieve this goal.

- Ask a neighbor.
- Ask a co-worker since you will probably have the same dental insurance.
- Contact a board certified oral surgeon (get the name from your local dental society or the yellow pages). They know who's good and who to shy away from. Ask for three names.
- Call each one and listen to how the staff answers the phone. Is it a warm welcoming greeting or are you an imposition on their time? Notice their response when you ask for a tour of their office. Do they seem surprised or are they instantly ready to invite you?
- When you take your tour make note of:
  o Did the dentist take the time to meet and greet you?
  o Cleanliness
  o Friendliness
  o Helpfulness
  o Age of the equipment and furnishings
  o Check out the dates on their reception area magazines. Are they current?
  o Check everyone's appearance.
  o Do they appear organized?
- Do they accept your dental insurance?
- What does your gut tell you? Will you be happy there?
- If you've answered yes then check them out with a checkup appointment.

Remember, even with insurance, you are paying this office and you should expect the appropriate care and attention all human beings deserve. And, yes, always listen to your gut. It never lies.

12

THE SINGING DENTIST RETURNS

"Singing is a way of escaping. It's another world.
I'm no longer on earth."
—EDITH PIAF

Remember these words from my mother? "You'll always have a career to fall back on if singing doesn't work out. You'll probably be known as the Singing Dentist." I can't help it. If I can't sing, then I can't work. I need music while I work. From the moment I started fixing teeth, I sang. Even in the operating room or the emergency room, I'd sing with the radio or tape player I brought with me. Patients always loved it. Not that I was such a vocal maestro, but more than that, it implied a sense of calm, a feeling that all is well and working out smoothly. Children also loved it. I'd use it to make them laugh. Actually, my mother didn't realize that I would combine both to make a career.

Here's a story. One week I had been getting phone calls from a Chicago company with a name I didn't recognize, and I kept forgetting to call them back. One evening, as I was getting ready to leave my office, my phone rang, and I answered it. It was that same Chicago-based company. It turns out that they were a publicity firm representing Wrigley gum. After many years of research, Wrigley had finally gained approval from the American Dental Association to market this gum, describing how it reduces cavities. Can you imagine chewing gum while preventing decay? To me it sounded a little incongruous, and I responded, "Why are you personally calling me with this information?"

"We want to get the message out to the public about this. After much discussion we thought it would be novel to have a dentist sing about the features and benefits of this gum across the country. We narrowed it down to three dentists. You are one of them."

Now this was interesting. "Give me greater details on what you would expect from me."

After much explanation and negotiation, they invited me to Chicago for a meeting with Wrigley. Subsequently, after I wrote a song on the benefits of preventive dentistry, I traveled around the country with my guitar and appeared on television and radio. The Singing Dentist had become my publicized moniker. You can check out one of these events online at http://www.passesdentalcare.com/fun- stuff/dr.-passes-on-tv.aspx. One time they had me singing in New York City, on the *Today Show* as well as *CBS This Morning*. Following that experience I and their whole crew went onto Broadway, literally, to sing my song. Here are some photographs of this event.

Me on the Great White Way singing to fight decay.

When the publicity campaign ended, I decided to keep up the Singing Dentist by appearing at various schools during Children's Dental Health Month in February. What great fun it was to do this. The kids loved it. But why am I telling you this? How can this possibly help my patients? Read on.

13

DISTRACTIVE DENTISTRY

"I need distractions. Good distractions, not bad ones.
A good distraction for me is a great play."
—DANNY AIELLO

"That's "You Will Be My Music" sung by Sinatra in his *Old Blue Eyes Is Back* album, 1973, written by Joe Raposo, arranged and conducted by Don Costa," stated Mr. Markham rather proudly. "But where's the music coming from?" He looked around the newly created treatment room.

"One of my greatest enjoyments is music. I love all kinds and have fun sharing this with my patients during their treatment. I installed a surround sound system in all of the treatment rooms for our listening pleasure. Two speakers are in the ceiling in front of the dental chair, and another two are behind you. It's connected to the computer where we can listen to just about any music you want through the Internet. That's how I was able to get this song for you. By the way, I'm very impressed that you knew all that information about that song," I said.

"I love that music. Nothing better than the old stuff. They don't write them like that today. Today it's nothing but noise."

And so our conversation went as I proceeded with his dental treatment while Mr. Markham forgot about his dental anxiety. So, what is the point to all of this? Two words: distractive dentistry.

It should be self-evident that you cannot be anxious and relaxed at the same time. It also follows that if you are distracted from some negative stimuli, your anxiety will not appear. My patient was so occupied with Sinatra and the wonderful sound system that he completely forgot about his dental treatment. As long as he didn't feel anything, he was humming and enjoying the music, not worrying about the dentistry.

Some years back, Diane Henderson needed to have a full-mouth reconstruction. This required the preparation and placement of twenty-eight crowns in her mouth. As you might quite well imagine, that was considerable treatment for your average patient. Unfortunately, Diane is not your average patient. She's a killer real estate broker with a persevering, overachieving, never-say-I-can't personality. She always gets the deal.

Her only issue is dentistry. To be more precise, she hates the dentist. (Thank God, I've had to deal with this my entire career, or she'd have eaten me alive.) I had to get her mind off dentistry, but how would I accomplish this?

While chatting I discovered that she loved Broadway shows. The following weekend she was going to see *Les Miserables*. Then it hit me.

"How would you like a preview of the play?" I asked her.

"What are you talking about? How can I do that?"

"What if I could play the entire score while I presented a verbal libretto of the play to you during treatment?"

"You know, that sounds better than you know. I usually buy the soundtrack of the play before I see it to familiarize myself with the play. I haven't had the time to get it. What a great idea. Thanks. Let's get going," she said in a commanding voice.

This was going to be a first for me. The curtain was going up while she opened up. As each scene was about to unfold, my clinical assistant paused the music, and I explained what was going on. Then the music resumed. She loved my visual descriptions of each scene. Distractive dentistry was at its best that afternoon and certainly deserved a Tony Award for the best off-off-off-Broadway performance. Not only was Diane wonderfully surprised at the stress-free nature of her treatment, she rewarded me by sending all of her new real estate clients to me.

ANALYSIS

Common sense

It's so simple that it should not need discussion. But it does, because most health professionals do not take the time to truly listen to their patients and then go the extra mile to satisfy their needs. All it took in both of these cases was to keep the patients away from their fears with a stronger positive stimulus. This works all the time. You can use it in other areas of your life.

14

A BETTER MOUSETRAP

"Focus, focus, focus."
—LL Cool J

When I had completed my first residency, I decided to pursue a second one in general anesthesia. What an amazing experience.

Every day at 7:00 a.m., I entered the operating room and prepared for the day's patients. Imagine being responsible for keeping someone alive and yet unconscious during their surgical procedure. This only strengthened my confidence building. My desire was to take this new skill to my office and treat the fearful patient under intravenous sedation. This residency would provide the proper credentials I needed to do this. Patients would schedule for root canals, extractions, or crown and bridge to be done while they were asleep. The concept was ideal, except for one small issue. I realized it as time went by. Let's learn more about this from Mrs. Frances Stromer.

"I'm your worst nightmare."

"Why is that?" I asked Francis.

"I don't even know you, and I hate you."

As if I'd never heard this before from a phobic patient, I answered nonchalantly, "Why is that?"

"You are going to hurt me, and I'm so fearful that I got diarrhea and the sweats just thinking about this visit last night."

Appreciating her candor, I asked, "How may I be of service to you?"

"Can you put me out and just pull my infected tooth?"

"Absolutely."

"Can you do it now?"

"Have you eaten anything since midnight, and is anyone here to take you home?"

"Nothing in the last eight hours, and my husband is here to take me home."

"Great. Then we can help you now."

I went through all of the preoperative medical history and informed consent procedures. Then we were ready to begin. She reclined in the dental chair, and my clinical assistant applied the tourniquet to her left arm. I was ready to insert the needle. As I was just about to do this, she took her other hand and pushed against my body with such unexpected strength that I almost fell over. Then, she jumped out of the chair while ripping the tourniquet off her arm. What happened next would have been comical if it hadn't been so tragic. She ran into the reception area, where there were patients calmly reading magazines, and at the top of her lungs she screamed, "I can't do this. You're killing me. Somebody help me! Help me!"

My assistant and I looked at each other dumbfounded. This I never expected. Her husband calmed her down. I escorted them into my private consultation room. After apologizing, she started to cry, explaining that she is also afraid to be out of control while sedated. That's when I realized what a great opportunity my Dental Anxiety Control Program would be for her. Let's return to the single flaw I discovered with intravenous sedation.

Patients would wake up thrilled that their dentistry was completed but would not return for a long time. Their fear was not addressed. Whatever prevented them from returning was still alive and, well, haunting them to avoid the dentist. A new way had to be created to allow people to return for routine care. These phobic dental patients did indeed return, but only after many years of neglect. Their mouths were filled, again, with decay, rot, and severe bleeding gum disease. This made no sense to me. Why spend all that money on proper care, under sedation, and then do it all over again? There had to be a better way.

My wife calls me MacGyver from that hit TV show in the eighties, in which he always came up with a way out of a dilemma. She admires my determination to always find a solution to a problem. This certainly was a world-class problem. After a bit of time, it hit me. As a teenager, I was fascinated with hypnosis. I learned how to perform it successfully on my classmates. What if there was a way to use this *and* advanced technology to help my patients? After much research I created a five-part program called the Dental Anxiety Control Program.

ANALYSIS

Here's how it works

The first visit consists of a **consultation** to learn what your story is; why you have so much dental anxiety and what triggers it. The second instructs the patient in **progressive relaxation**. This technique enables you, the patient, to easily and quickly relax yourself when you feel unnecessarily stressed. At a moment's notice, you will be able to replace stress and anxiety with comfortable feelings of relaxation. The third visit involves learning how to use **biofeedback**. This helps you to spot when your muscles are tightening up, leading to stress and anxiety. Both of these steps are practiced at home with easy-to-use portable equipment. The fourth visit brings progressive relaxation and biofeedback together to **desensitize** you to your fear. It could be the dental injection, the sound of the drill, or anything else, for that matter. Desensitization allows you to feel more comfortable with past negative memories of dental treatment. The fifth and last part to your dental anxiety control is **graduation day**. On this visit we incorporate all of the steps as you start dental treatment. All of this has proved to be most effective.

Francis decided to undergo this process with much success. Indeed, it was so successful that she had her tooth saved with root canal therapy instead of extraction. This procedure became such an indelible part of her life that, years later, when she discovered that she had breast cancer, she applied the same techniques to help her with her surgery. She phoned me after her surgery, explaining how well it helped her cope with that ordeal. These are the moments that I live for.

My creation of this procedure was so successful that I became the director of the Dental Anxiety Control Center at Jamaica Hospital. Doctors would travel to us learning how to use this skill in their practice. Now people no longer would need intravenous drugs. Instead they would learn how to become a routine patient, on a routine basis, keeping their teeth routinely cared for in a less costly manner. Now, this made sense to me. Then, I found the next flaw in the process.

Though effective, the Dental Anxiety Control Program took too long. Patients might spend five weeks pursuing this program until positive results were attained. A faster way had to be found. Then it hit me. Why not spend more time with patients during their first consultation, digging out their stories? A more personal intimate dialogue would be had between them, me and a staff member. To be more concise, we were developing instant rapport within an accelerated track. Patients reacted quite well to this and have proceeded with treatment immediately.

To this day, I have abided by this philosophy with all my patients. In this twenty-first century, when our lives have become cloaked in a cocoon of technology, where we seem to be farther apart, less intimate with each other, as smartphones build a wall to personal contact, my patients find it refreshing to feel the attention of caring human interest directed toward them. Deep down, this is what we all want, especially from a provider of intimate services such as dentistry. Now my patients are released from their self-imposed mental prison sentence of dental stress and anxiety.

To see the entire process of the Dental Anxiety Program log onto: http://www. passesdentalcare.com/fun-stuff/dr.- passes-on-tv.aspx.

DENTAL TIP:

Implant Care

Just because you have implants don't believe that you have become bionic and cannot suffer the ravages of bacterial invasion. Implants are artificial roots but their surrounding structures are human. They are part of you. Your bone and gums can become destroyed from neglect. Infection, inflammation and recession of your bone and gums can cause these implants to become lose and fall out. Perform appropriate oral preventive procedures described elsewhere in this book. Be sure to have your teeth examined and cleaned at least twice a year by your dentist or hygienist. Also, x-ray examination is essential in diagnosing periodontal disease around your implants. Be true to your teeth or they will be false to you!

15

SAME-DAY DENTISTRY

"Procrastination is the bad habit of putting off
until the day after tomorrow what should have been
done the day before yesterday."
—NAPOLEON HILL

Now the title of this chapter seems like an absurd redundancy. Of course all dentistry is done the same day. That's like saying, "Fillings done while you wait." Is there any other way to do them? But if you dig deeper you'll discover that this title has greater meaning than is apparent at first glance. Let's explore this most beneficial service in the form of a story.

It is ten thirty in the morning. The office telephone rings. Meena answers it, "Passes Dental Care. Meena speaking. How may I serve you?"

"This is Cathy Wu. I just broke my front tooth. I have a meeting with my son's teacher tonight. I will be very embarrassed if I have to go to that meeting looking like this. Please can you help me? It's very important."

"Of course we will help you. Are you a patient of our practice?" Meena asked.

"No. I moved into the neighborhood recently and have no dentist. But please can you help me today?" Cathy implored.

"Absolutely. We'll do everything in our power to help you."

"Thank goodness. When can I come in?"

"Does one o'clock work for you?"

"I'll be there. You don't know how much I appreciate this. Thank you so much. I mean, you don't even know me, and you're willing to help me. Thank you so much."

"You would do the same for me if our situations were reversed," Meena concluded.

"Yes, I would. I'll see you at one."

That certainly sounds like a reasonable circumstance. Now, let's look at this a little differently.

"How long have you had this broken tooth?" Sara, my hygienist, asked Mrs. Longworth while cleaning her teeth.

"What broken tooth?" she answered, shocked. "Your upper right first molar has a cusp fractured. Here let me show you," Sara replied in a helpful fashion.

Sara took out her pen-like digital camera and took a photograph of the dental mishap. After snapping the picture, Sara opened the image on her computer monitor in the treatment room.

"Take a look at this. Here is where the cusp of your tooth should be. Clearly you can see that it is fractured off. If the tooth is not restored properly you will need a root canal procedure," Sara stated quite plainly.

"Oh, my gosh! That looks horrible. I had no idea. I never felt anything. What should we do?"

"I'll get Dr. Passes to come in and give us a second opinion. He'll have the final word on it."

After being alerted to the problem, I told Mrs. Longworth that we could place a filling in the tooth, and she could be on her way. She was advised to speak with Sara about setting the appointment.

"You're here now. If we could do the filling for you now, would you like to stay?" Sara asked.

"That would be great. I'm a teacher, so my time is taken up with my family and school. Getting this fixed now would be a great time saver for me. I'll stay," she said rather gratefully.

The two stories are similar, yet different. The dissimilarities are the circumstances in which the appointments are being made. Cathy Wu called for an immediate concern needing urgent attention. Mrs. Longworth stepped into an almost urgent circumstance unexpectedly. Being accommodating to her time, in this instance, proved to have great value to her.

It is my deep-seated opinion that my staff should do all that is necessary to help people with same-day dentistry as the need arises. This is a special service, and we have to move our schedule around in order to accommodate unexpected dental situations. Same-day dentistry is sound, solid service supplying supportive specialized solutions, stretching the spell of time to suit the necessities of the patient. (Forgive me for playing the role of an adventurous alliterative author. It seemed like a fun thing to do.)

Basically, we'll do all we can to provide you with treatment in a timely fashion as quickly as possible. That's the way it should be.

16

MR. PRESIDENT AND LEADERSHIP SKILLS

"You do not lead by hitting people over the head—that's assault, not leadership."
—DWIGHT D. EISENHOWER

As I entered private practice, I became interested in developing and sharpening my leadership skills. The most natural arena to hone this edge was on the grinding stone of politics. Realizing that there was much more to dentistry than just filling a hole, I became active in my local dental association, Queens County Dental Society (QCDS). As usual, there was a climb up the ladder within the organization. I spent many years as a member of its board of directors learning what it takes to become a leader. During this time, I chaired many activities within the context of continuing dental education for our more than one thousand member dentists. One of my favorite programs was the annual cardiopulmonary resuscitation (CPR) recertification course. Every April, the dental societies of Queens County, Nassau County, and Suffolk County joined forces to form a large educational conference called the Greater Long Island Dental Meeting. Having obtained my Advanced Cardiac Life Support (ACLS) certification, I chaired the CPR program. We spent a full day instructing dentists and staff on the details of CPR. It was highly significant for me, since I used intravenous sedation in my practice.

One day, after many years of dental society involvement, I found myself being nominated for secretary. This was the first rung on the proverbial ladder to the presidency. As the years unfolded, I finally found myself staring at this august position within my organization. At the time, I was the youngest person to ever assume this office. In connection with this position, I also became president of the Institute on Continuing Dental Education. Here's where it gets interesting.

In January of 1988 there was the inauguration of the new slate of officers. The president has the honor of selecting the presiding official to perform this ceremony. After much thought I suggested that the U.S. attorney for the southern district of New York performs this honor. This was Rudy Giuliani. You need to know that he had made a name for himself by cleaning up crime of all kinds in the New York City area. Since he had designs on becoming the mayor of New York City, I felt that he would be agreeable to my invitation. It was uplifting to read his letter of acceptance.

The night of the inauguration, Rudy and I spent an hour together discussing its agenda. What a delightful and funny person he was, with a lighthearted and full sense of good humor. I introduced him to the few hundred gathered members as "the modern day Elliot Ness." Upon hearing this he raised his eyebrows and for a second became dumbfounded. To the audience he said, "Harvey, I don't know that I fit in Ness's stature, but I am thrilled to be in the same sentence as him."

The following page shows a photograph of two younger and goofy-looking guys trying to do some good in this world.

After that evening we had spoken a few times more as I watched his ascent into the politics of New York. Many years later, as life progressed, we met up for breakfast before a common meeting. Photographers were there to snap some photos of us. During some of the time spent with Rudy, I asked him questions regarding leadership. His answers and advice were always to the point and highly valuable.

Hey! What happened to our hair?

Leadership is a funny kind of thing. To me, it's that rare skill that needs to be taught by learning from others. True, I have read numerous books on the subject, but nothing equals the personal touch in observing or listening to another more skilled individual.

As a dental student, I spent many years shadowing my mentors. To this day, if I find someone who has much to offer me, I always ask if he/she would be my mentor. Their age, occupation, or any other factor is irrelevant to me. A most important mentor to me was Walter Haley, a retired oil magnate and manager of John Connally's campaign for governor of Texas. Governor Connally, while seated in the jump seat of the car, was the other person shot in the Kennedy assassination. During Walter's retirement, he created another enterprise, instructing dentists on how to run their business. One of the many things Walter taught me was that my life is my corporation. Every good corporation needs a board of directors to advise its president. As you go through life, you will meet people whom you should invite to be on your board of directors, advising you on certain subjects. You would be amazed at the number of seemingly unreachable people who agree to support and advise you. How would *you* feel if someone requested your advice? I'd bet on your helping them.

DENTAL TIP:

Dentists detect Osteoporosis in Women?

Your dentist may be the first to detect this condition through a routine dental examination and x-rays. If you are over 50 he will look for:

- *Tooth loss*
- *Bone loss within your jaws*
- *Poor fitting dentures that need to be replaced frequently.*

All of this is due to the decrease in bone density within your jaw bones from osteoporosis. Your dentist should refer you to your physician to diagnose your condition. You can help to prevent this by ingesting enough calcium during the day. Men should take 800mg while women should take 1,200mg daily. Once you pass 65 up your dose to 1,500mg daily. Add vitamin D as well. Cut back on your alcohol and caffeine while you also quit smoking. Resistance exercising is a great help.

So remember, the next time someone calls you a bonehead thank them.

17

INTO THE ARMS OF MORPHEUS

"I reached for sleep and drew it round me like a blanket
muffling pain and thought together in the merciful dark."
—MARY STEWART

"You don't seem to understand," Tim McInerny said while nervously wiping the sweat from his forehead. "I am not interested in getting rid of this fear. I do not have the time or inclination to do anything about it. If you could put me to sleep and fix my teeth, I'd be thrilled."

To be brutally honest with you, I must state that sometimes no matter what I say to patients they will still not want to rid themselves of this emotional affliction. It's like talking to the wall. Nothing gets through. In that circumstance, I go back into the box, only this time I pull out a different trick to help them.

If you remember, one of my original areas of training was in general anesthesia. I would insert an intravenous line and administer a sedative to relax the patient while producing amnesia to their treatment. There are those people who still request and need this type of care. In the seventies and eighties, it was a common protocol for most dentists using sedation in their practices to function as the anesthetist as well as the operating dentist. We would restore teeth while concomitantly monitoring the sedated patient's vital signs of heart rate, depth and rate of respiration, and oxygen saturation (by watching for any bluish discoloration on the bed of the fingernails or skin pallor).

Today, when I think about those methods of the past, I shudder to realize what problems all of us could have encountered. It was considered an acceptable way to practice. Fortunately, my philosophy has changed for the benefit of the patient. I now enlist the assistance of a licensed dental anesthesiologist. In the outpatient dental office, this highly experienced doctor will offer the same service provided to gastroenterologists performing colonoscopies or endoscopies. The patient comes out of the procedure with no recollection of it. After inducing sedation the dental anesthesiologist will monitor the patient's vital signs while I concentrate on their dentistry. *Each area of specialization unto himself* is my motto.

As I mentioned earlier, there are still those who will benefit from this type of service. They do not wish to release themselves from their mental bondage of dental fear. What better way to help them than to use a licensed dental anesthesiologist?

ANALYSIS

It never pays to argue with someone over what they want. You can never win. Exerting your will over another is foolish and a waste of time. In the end, give them what they want. Remember, it's not what the patient says that counts. It's what they do. And they will leave the office to go to another dentist who will give them what they want. That's why it is important for the dentist to learn many skills within a large inventory of services to offer the patient.

18

Do This to Save Your Teeth

"May the floss be with you."
(Or something like that.)
—Apologies to Obi-Wan Kenobi, *Star Wars Trilogy*

"Why am I getting such decay all of a sudden?" Lucy asked me.

"It's not all of a sudden," I replied. "What do you mean? We haven't seen you for years. During that time your mouth was not watched over by us. My hygienist did not give you a cleaning and bacterial by-products built up in your mouth along the teeth and gums."

With raised eyebrows, Lucy asked, "It happens that fast?"

"Lucy, you need to realize how quickly bacteria can claim destruction to your mouth. Besides, it's no secret that you should return for your checkups and cleanings at least twice a year, not once every four years."

"Please understand that I was afraid to come in due to the downturn in the economy."

"I hear that a lot. People need to understand that the cost of a checkup and cleaning is minimal considering the cost to fix the bacterial destruction. Besides, most insurance companies pay 100 percent of the preventive costs anyway. They know that it is cheaper to prevent a problem than to fix it."

"During this recession I guess I haven't been thinking clearly. I'm mostly thinking in terms of fear," Lucy said.

"I was amazed at how much dentistry needs to be done now because of all the self-imposed neglect people have done to themselves," I said.

"But how does all of this happen? What exactly causes this breakdown? I brush my teeth daily. How could this happen?" Lucy asked rather intensely.

"There will always be bacteria living in your mouth. There's no escaping this fact. And after they eat the food you leave behind, they excrete waste, which is acidic, in your mouth. It is this acid that robs your teeth of minerals. These minerals are responsible for creating the enormous strength that provides your teeth with its structural integrity. But the smallest living creatures on earth have the ability to destroy the second-hardest naturally occurring substance on earth: tooth enamel."

"What's the hardest? I mean the first one," Lucy asked.

"A diamond," I replied.

Watching her eyes drift upward and to her left, I saw her pensive gaze as she simply stated, "Wow. That is hard. Okay, so I get that. But how could I have prevented this condition if I'm already brushing my teeth every day?"

"It's real simple and inexpensive. First, you have to come in at least twice a year for a good cleaning and checkup."

"Why? I mean what exactly happens? I like details, so please take your time in answering me," Lucy said.

"You might find this information interesting. At the University of Pennsylvania School of Dental Medicine, a study was conducted to understand how this works. After a dental cleaning the bacterial colonies that existed are destroyed. The number of bacteria drops precipitously. You can never get rid of them entirely, but their quantities would now be at a level causing minimal destruction to your teeth and gums."

"That makes sense, but for how long?" she asked while finding herself becoming more engaged in this topic.

"You're beginning to get the picture. Let me continue. The researchers discovered that it takes seventy-two to ninety days for the bacteria to regroup and begin to recolonize. If you don't get a cleaning after that time bacterial destruction starts all over again in your mouth. They excrete their poisonous toxins in your mouth, causing bleeding, gum and bone loss, bad breath, decay, and much more."

Putting the brakes on this rhythm, Lucy interrupted me, "Wait a minute. You said that I should have a cleaning every six months. Now it sounds like it should be every three months. Which is it?"

"You are a detail-oriented person, Lucy. You picked up on that real fast. Here's the problem. Most people should have their cleanings every three months. The problem is the insurance companies. They will not give you more that two cleanings a year. And that is what people have come to expect. It's all about the financial aspects of health care."

Pondering this for a few seconds, she then replied, "I don't care what the insurance companies do. I get it and want my cleanings every three months. Considering the benefits, the cost is minimal."

Feeling good about the results of my dental evangelistic sermon, I continued with, "My staff and I need to examine your teeth, bone, and gums twice a year. We also need to periodically check your bite and perform an oral cancer screening exam. Those patients who maintain this schedule have the least amount of dentistry to be done. It truly works."

"Your hygienists have always been so gentle and pleasant to be with," Lucy added.

"They completed their certification requirements to be able to give you numbing injections or laughing gas, if you should want this. They had to take postgraduate courses for this skill and service. I'm proud to say that they are quite good at this," I said with a satisfied smile on my face.

"As for cosmetics, most people just need to have their stains removed on a regular basis. My hygienists will also explain which foods are chromogenic or stain producing to your teeth. Just by keeping your teeth clean will be enough to enhance your smile."

"I'm using a regular toothbrush. Is there something better for me to use?" she asked.

"I prefer the electric toothbrushes over the manual traditional types. The issue is that you need to brush each quarter of your mouth for thirty seconds. Two minutes in its entirety. My hygienists can show you how to use them. Some models come with various bristle heads to clean out your teeth effectively."

"By the way, I heard you mention something about a cosmetic cleaning to another patient in the reception area. What is that?"

"A cosmetic cleaning is something I conceived. This incorporates all of the necessary aspects of a routine dental cleaning but adds whitening of selected teeth where stubborn stains cannot be removed, or the tooth is just too dark. It adds the best of everything."

"This is great stuff. Let me schedule an appointment with Sara for my hygiene visit. Then I'm sure you'll tell me what needs to be done for my teeth to get back into health. I won't let this happen again. Thanks for taking the time to explain this to me. I feel like I've just spent a day in dental school," she said.

"My pleasure. And, remember, may the floss be with you."

She just laughed politely while rolling her eyes up to heaven in response to my corny humor.

(I realize that you read this information earlier as a dental tip. It is included in this chapter because of its vital importance to you. This is the key to maintaining optimal oral health. Amazing as it might sound, most people refuse to partake in this most simple yet vital routine exercise. I hope you will.)

19

PEARLY WHITES

"I want the whitest teeth possible."
—EVERYONE

"I hear so much about tooth whitening. Is it right for me?" Loni Cook inquired.

"How much time do you have for my answer?" I said half joking.

"I'm off today. Take all the time you need. I'm truly interested in this."

"Well, to start with, whitening or bleaching your teeth begins with proper diagnosis and then appropriate treatment planning."

"What do you mean? I thought it was just a simple process and that's the end of it."

"Here's what I mean. To start with, I need to examine your teeth. Did you know that not all teeth are created equal? Teeth have three major shades of staining. The first has a yellowish hue to it. That's the least difficult stain to bleach. This follows with a brownish hue. This becomes more challenging for us to whiten. It just takes a little more time to accomplish. Then comes the most difficult stain to lighten. That's the grayish stain. This stain is usually a result of either a genetic condition or the result of tetracycline staining after this antibiotic was administered in childhood, during the development of your teeth."

"What do you do for gray-stained teeth?"

"First we try to lighten it. It may brighten somewhat but it never gets to the level that satisfies the patient. That's when we consider bonding or porcelain laminate veneers."

"Wow. This is getting quite complicated. I thought that this would be simple," Loni conceded.

"Actually, it's rather simple. The dentist and hygienist are your experts in this field and can usually make a snap judgment just by looking."

"Let's get back to me. I want whiter teeth. What can you do for me?" she asked.

"You're in luck. You have a yellowish stain, which will be the least challenging to whiten."

"How do you do it? I mean what is the process like? Will it hurt? How long will it take? Will the stains come back?" Loni asked enthusiastically.

"Whoa. Slow down. One of my hygienists is here today and performs the bleaching procedure. She will go over all of this with you before she starts. Shall I ask her to come in and speak to you?"

"Yes. Cara's great. She's always been so gentle." Cara's warm smile greeted Loni as she entered the treatment room. "Hi, Loni. Dr. P. tells me that you want whiter teeth."

"I do. When can we begin?"

"I need to present a full description of the procedure before we begin. It's called informed consent. There are just a few things you need to know," Cara said.

"Like what?"

"I know that Dr. Passes explained some things to you but there's more to tell you."

"Okay. Tell me," Loni said.

"We use a highly effective system called Zoom. It seems to produce the greatest increase in whiteness to the teeth. This bleaching process works only on natural teeth. It will not whiten fillings or crowns. If you have any fillings, then Dr. Passes can replace them with whiter ones after the process is completed, if needed. This is rarely needed. Remember, that's only for the front teeth. Also, if you have any small fracture lines within your teeth they could become sensitive for a few hours afterward. This rarely happens here. Years ago, Dr. Passes discovered that if he gave patients some fluoride to rinse their teeth with before and then after the process, this sensitivity rarely occurs. It seems that the fluoride protects the teeth like an overcoat on your body in the winter."

"How long does the whitening process take?" Loni asked.

"It takes about two hours. We must clean your teeth first. There cannot be any foreign material on your teeth or the bleaching gel will not be able to touch the tooth's surface."

"What exactly is the process like? How do you do it?"

"First, we apply a protective barrier to your gums. Then some whitening gel is placed on your teeth. A laserlike light is then shone on this gel. The gel is activated and starts the whitening process. We do this only to the areas on your teeth that are visible to others. The backs of your teeth are not whitened either. Afterward, we may give you a take-home kit to continue the whitening process if it is felt that you would benefit from it. What's interesting is that we discovered that the whitening process continues for about forty-eight hours. So during this time, do not consume any chromogenic food or drink. It's all rather straightforward."

"What's chromogenic?" Loni asked.

"Oh, I'm sorry. That means color producing, like red wine, tomato sauce, or grape juice. And do not smoke."

"I don't smoke, but I do enjoy red wine."

"Well, for next two days, you'll enjoy white wine," Cara said with a wink. "The good news is that our patients are happy with their whiter smiles. It's amazing how much confidence one gets with a whiter smile."

Cara continued to explain that she would give Loni a whitening take-home kit to enhance the whitening process.

With a wide smile of acceptance, Loni said, "When can we start?"

"Right now, if you are ready," Cara replied with unabated enthusiasm.

And so, another beaming smile entered our world.

20

PORCELAIN LAMINATE VENEERS

"Love of beauty is taste. The creation of beauty is art."
—RALPH WALDO EMERSON

With a hopeful glimmer in her eyes, Tina stated bluntly, "It's been my greatest wish to have beautiful teeth."

"Please tell me more. I need to understand why," I asked her.

Tina was an immaculately dressed teacher who took obvious pride in her appearance. Her clothes, hairstyling, and manicured presence attested to this. Though she was sixty years old, her skin was not marred by the lines of age. All was lovely to the eye, except when she opened her mouth to smile. As expected, her hand went up to cover it. When she finally allowed me to see what the condition of her smile was, I appreciated her concern. One of her front teeth was forward and covering the other. The crowding of her other teeth assisted in her mangled dental visage.

"I know it's a small thing, but when I want to smile I feel great embarrassment and hold off expressing joy on my face. It's been this way as far back as I can remember."

I waited for her revealing story to conclude before I expressed mine. "Tina, this is one of my absolute favorite things to do in dentistry. Would you like to see and hear what your cosmetic options are?"

"Most definitely."

I took photos of her teeth and had my staff create a digital cosmetic smile makeover for her to see. All of her teeth were digitally moved into a more harmonious position through computerization while whitening them. She then followed me to the computer monitor as we gazed at her before and after photos. "Wow," was all she could utter, which finally followed with, "How do we do this?"

"Here are your choices. As I see it, there are two solid ways to accomplish this. Clear aligner therapy, which you know as Invisalign, coupled with teeth whitening or just porcelain laminate veneers. Or a combination of both services."

Invisalign is a virtually invisible tooth straightening procedure used to move misaligned teeth into a more periodontal favorable position. It allows for better dental health when the teeth are aligned as nature intended. Clear aligner therapy helps to prevent the collision of teeth, which can produce receding gums and bone loss. After this alignment is achieved, the teeth can be whitened to improve their appearance. If the patient is not happy with the shape of her teeth then porcelain laminate veneers could be placed over them to provide the best shape and color possible.

Tina thought this over and stated that she did not want to spend the extended time with Invisalign. She wanted a beautiful smile as soon as possible. I explained that porcelain laminate veneers have the ability to change the shape of the teeth, creating an appearance as if she had them aligned with orthodontic treatment.

"It seems to me that I could get the look I'm after with just porcelain laminate veneers in a shorter period of time for less cost, without using Invisalign. Don't you agree?" Tina asked.

"You're right, and it will take just two visits per jaw arch. Would you like to see how this procedure is done?"

"How? Do you have a patient here right now who is having this done?"

"Well, not exactly. We can go to my Web site and watch a short video demonstrating how it's done. It will show you the whole procedure. Want to see it?"

"Absolutely."

I clicked on http://www.passesdentalcare.com/fun- stuff/dr.-passes-on-tv.aspx. You can do the same thing to see what Tina saw. It's a great informational tool. The part demonstrating the porcelain veneers is about twelve minutes into the show.

Tina agreed, and when we finished her smile makeover, she felt like a new woman.

"It feels like I have a new formal evening gown on all the time. I can't get over the way I feel. My husband even told me that it was a marvelous improvement in my appearance. The funny part is that my colleagues at school said that I looked really good but didn't know what had changed. The enhancement was so subtle; no one realized that it was my teeth."

"I'm so happy for you. And now you know why I love doing this more than anything else for patients. Thanks for allowing me to do this. I am grateful for the opportunity. It means a lot to me."

21

IT'S SO EASY TO BE SUCCESSFUL.

"Give people what they want,
and they will give you what you want."
—ZIG ZIGLAR

My intent is not to be arrogant in this chapter's title. Rather, it is observing Zig Ziglar's famous quote. Allow me to share a story that changed my perspective on how I see my practice helping people.

One day I called my physician's office for an appointment. "Doctor's office," was the not-so-welcoming greeting I heard from the other end of the phone.

"Hi. This is Harvey Passes. I'd like to make an appointment."

"The doctor can see you next Thursday at two thirty."

"I see patients at that time. Is there anything available before or after my work hours?"

"No. Our hours are nine to four. You'll have to find the time to come in during those hours."

Feeling stuck between a rock and a hard place, I hung up without making an appointment. I sat in my chair and had another of my epiphanies. I've been doing the same stupid thing to my patients. How can working people take the time to come in for cleanings or checkups during the day when they have to earn their daily bread or go to school? I decided to change my hours to accommodate working people or students. Instead of seeing patients in the time that was convenient for me, I changed it to those hours that were more available for working people. People now visit us between 7:00 a.m. and 7:00 p.m. I'm always thrilled when I see someone in the chair during those hours, and they share their happiness at being seen so conveniently.

My other epiphany was the insurance conundrum. Then it hit me. Here's another story to make my point.

Mrs. Froum called and explained that she was a new patient. She wanted to know if we took her insurance. My staff member said that we did. Mrs. Froum stated that my name was not on her list of insurance member dentists. How could we possibly take her insurance?

Staff replied with true out-of-the-box thinking. "We do not need to be a member of your plan to take your insurance. We will honor most insurance companies' fees as if we were on your plan. This way we do not have to be caught up in the insurance company bureaucratic red tape. Patients are now happy to know that their insurance will work with us while maintaining excellent quality care."

As the chapter title states, it is easy to be successful. There is no magic bullet. Just do the right thing. Give people what they want, and they will come to you.

22

EXPEDODONTICS

"Innovation distinguishes between a leader and a follower."
—STEVE JOBS

"Why is this taking so long?" asked Ryan Murray.
"There are steps that I must go through to create your bridge. Unfortunately, it just takes time to do it right," I replied.

Frowning, he replied, "I don't get it. We can now go to Mars, create artificially moving body parts, speak to anyone around the world on our cell phones, even see them on the phone, and you're telling me that dentistry cannot find a way to speed up this crown and bridge process?"

Caught like a deer in his headlights I just stared at him without much to say. Seeing my thoughtless gaze, Mr. Murray continued, with just a little more sensitive consideration, "I know that you're a truly bright guy. Why don't you figure out a way to expedite it? Do you know how many businesspeople would be eager to come to you for quicker service? Time is everything to us. I know that I would."

Deep in thought, I answered, "You know, Ryan, I think I will do something about this."

"Good. Now, come on with fitting my bridge. I've gotta get out of here for an important meeting in the city."

I discussed this with many of my local labs. My offering suggestions to them on how we might speed up the process only brought conservative replies and fruitless answers. Upon thoughtful reflection, I began to realize how "stuck in the mud" these local labs were. All they wanted to do was status quo. All were afraid to break out of the box.

"If we expedite your dentistry, and it doesn't fit, who's going to take the hit on it when it needs to be redone?" was one response. Another was, "It's impossible to do what you want. You can't leave out all of the steps." And on and on it went. Frustration became an unwelcomed companion of mine during these conversations. Then it all turned around.

During a continuing education course in Phoenix, Arizona, a dentist was presenting his latest concepts in patient care when he mentioned the name of a lab that expedited treatment. The lab was not intimidated by this accelerated process and professed to deliver accurate cosmetic prosthetics. I wrote down their phone number.

Heikas, my future lifelong friend and technician, answered his phone. After brief pleasantries, I inquired if he was able to create crowns and bridges in less time than it took in most labs. In a reassuring tone, he said that not only could he do it but would guarantee his workmanship for five years. My local labs would only give dentists one year. Dentures are usually warranted locally for one year as well. He would honor a two-year commitment for them.

What impressed me even more was his willingness to experiment with me in providing new techniques for faster service while maintaining quality without increasing costs. His pledge to explore with me was most unusual. Together, through the years, we have developed amazing techniques to make people smile.

Let's get technical and go cordless

In order to provide a natural appearance and an accurately fitting crown under the gum, one must create a small space under the gum 360° around the tooth. This way, the laboratory will be able to see exactly where to end the crown under the gum. Traditionally, the dentist places a string like cord impregnated with a hemostatic chemical preventing bleeding. Its placement is painful and time-consuming. Even if local anesthetic is given, there is usually postoperative discomfort about the gums as well as bleeding. Placing the old fashioned retraction cord under the gums also results in greater bleeding that covers the tooth, preventing reliable impressions of the tooth for the lab.

Through much experimentation, I have created a faster, more accurate, and kinder technique to provide the lab with a means to finish the case quicker. I simply take a special dental bur, place it about a millimeter under the gum, and rotate it 360° about the tooth. This temporarily opens the space with virtually no bleeding or postoperative discomfort. It enables the impression material to go under the gums for an accurate representation of the tooth. This will provide the lab with astounding accuracy in order to create excellently fitting crowns.

Let's revisit Mr. Murray.

Years later, after I had achieved great success in expediting dental treatment, Mr. Murray appeared, needing to have many teeth crowned. Not only was there decay, but he wanted an improved appearance in his smile.

Not missing a beat, he opened with exactly what I knew would be his first question. It had nothing to do with money or final results. He asked in an almost accusatory fashion and with not a little bit of sarcasm, "So how long will this take?"

"The routine number of visits this treatment normally takes." Then I paused to choose my words to him before pleasantly shocking him. "Let's see, the first visit I prepare ten teeth, take the impression, and create temporary teeth and a bite registration. The second visit we try in the individual castings and take a connection registration. The third visit I try in the connections and check the fit. The fourth visit I try in the raw porcelain and check your bite. The fifth visit I insert the case with temporary cement, and you go home with it. If there are any inaccuracies, then we have to do that visit over again. Treatment could take five to six visits or more if I have the lab redo anything. Since this case is very challenging, it might take seven to nine visits." Then I waited for his expected reply.

"You've got to be kidding me. I remember asking you if there was any way to expedite treatment, and you just stared at me. Dentistry can't improve on this?" Murray asked with not a little bit of disgust.

"How would you like it completed in just two visits?"

"What are you saying?"

"Just that. What if I could provide the same service in just two visits? Would that satisfy your need for expediency?"

Eyes wide open, he said, "How is that possible from what you've just told me?"

Then I related what I had done to respond to his suggestion made years before. With a rather impressed attitude, he said, "When can we begin?"

Then he remembered something. "Oh, I just recalled those damn cords you placed under my gums before the impression. That is the only obstacle I have in moving forward. That was horrible. And what a bloody mess it was when I rinsed out. I hated that pressure feeling under my gums afterward. Let me give this some thought."

"Ryan," I continued with much exuberant enthusiasm, "I truly listened to you years ago. That no longer exists."

"You're kidding. Then how do you take the impression under the gum for an accurate fit?" he asked, bewildered.

"Because you are one of my few patients with a sincere curiosity who loves to solve challenges, and you won't get bored, I will get technical with you. While looking for a more expedient process, I came across a new impression material that would allow me to shorten the treatment time. Here's how it works."

I proceeded to explain my discovery to Murray. "I found that if I place a certain dental bur about one to two millimeters under the gum, three hundred and sixty degrees around the tooth, a small, virtually dry space is created. This space remains open for a short period of time. Immediately, I insert in the mouth this new impression material. It starts out with the consistency of mayonnaise but sets to the hardness of plaster. Another innovation is the type of tray I use to deliver this material. This tray gives me an amazingly accurate impression of both jaws at the same time. After it sets, I place a secondary, more watery, flowable impression material within the first impression and put it back into the mouth. The plaster-like first material pushes the more flowable material under the gums in the small space, capturing the tooth's shape under the gum. There are no painful cords to place and nothing to quickly remove. It is a streamlined, more accurate, stress-free procedure than what is used by all of my colleagues. Only because I am so fastidious about my dentistry, I take a second bite so that the lab will be able to confirm accuracy. This provides all the information the lab needs to create magnificent, well-fitting cosmetic crowns without that black line running along the gums."

Nearly speechless, Murray just responded with a pensive, "Hmm," followed by, "I'm impressed. Makes sense to me."

His case was completed within two and a half weeks. The final case was tried in with minimal adjustments. Murray left happy and most comfortable. "My anxiety over time has left me. I knew you could do it." As he was leaving the office, he abruptly turned around and said to me, "Why not call this faster, more accurate treatment expedodontics?"

Chuckling, I answered that I would give it some thought. I began to see other areas in dentistry that could benefit from this expedodontics concept. How could I expedite fillings?

Thanking him, I realized that my constant companion of frustration had left me. I felt a lift to my spirits.

ANALYSIS

It's Too Hard to Do!

You can never give up. As I always tell my children when they state that something is hard to do, hard just means it takes longer to do. There is always a solution to a problem. You just have to keep looking deeper with great perseverance. In this case, Mr. Murray threw down the gauntlet with a valid challenge. Many patients have complained through the years about how long some treatments could be. This made sense to pursue. In trying to solve this dilemma, I needed to find a partner who was willing to take chances with me. I had to develop new clinical techniques that would allow the lab to accelerate treatment. The old way wouldn't work.

DENTAL TIP:

Dental Sealants

Dental sealants are an excellent way to prevent tooth decay in children. The dental sealant procedure takes only minutes, is painless, is much less than half the cost of a filling, and is virtually 100 percent effective at stopping decay. Insurance companies will make benefits available for their use in children. There are times when adults could benefit from this service. I usually discuss this with my patients on an individual basis in order to determine if this is appropriate for them.

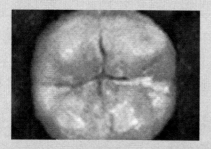

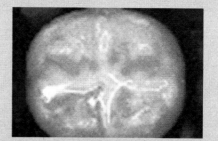

Before Sealant   **After Sealant**

23

QUICKSILVER: FRIEND OR FOE?

*"Cowardice asks: Is it safe? Expediency asks: Is it politic? But
Conscience asks: Is it right?"*
—WILLIAM PUNSHON

Since its creation, the mercury filling, or the dental amalgam, has been a source
of severe controversy among dentists and patients.

There is evidence indicating that this kind of filling was used in China around
700 to 900 AD and in Germany during the early fifteen hundreds. Ever since the
eighteen thirties, the amalgam restoration has been the subject of constant controversy, due to its mercury content. Indeed, mercury poisoning can cause brain,
kidney, lung, and other organ illnesses.

This material was made by mixing approximately 50 percent mercury with the
filings of silver coins. During the early eighteen hundreds, American dentists had to
sign a pledge that they would not use it for their patients. This was abandoned when
the American Dental Association (ADA) was founded in the eighteen fifties. Until
this very day their position has been that the mercury amalgam filling is a safe effective restoration for children and adults. Yet, there are countries that disagree and
have outlawed its use for their citizens. What follows next is where it truly became
nonsensical and outright dumb.

One morning I read in the *ADA Newsletter* how studies with the Food and Drug
Administration (FDA) had concluded that no evidence existed proving that the mercury amalgam filling was dangerous to health. Later that very same day, I received

a notification from the state of New York, instructing dentists to install, at their own expense, a mercury trap within their water-waste system. This was legislated to capture all of the mercury filling material that was suctioned out of patients' mouths during treatment. It stated that the legislature of New York State did not want mercury in the state's water drainage system. Periodically, a hazmat (hazardous material) company had to come to the dental office to collect these containers and dispose of them properly.

The absurdity of this became more evident when I thought how the federal government and the ADA stated that mercury fillings are safe in your mouth yet the state of New York does not want it in our water drainage system. Why should it be safe to put into your mouth but not safe to spit out into the drainage? Something did not make sense here.

I have always believed that these restorations should not be my first choice, and indeed I have not used them for more than thirty years. I wouldn't use them for my family or for any of my patients.

We are living in a technically advanced era in which dentistry has made amazing strides. What substitute exists to replace the mercury filling? Bonding is the answer.

Bonding is a process using a plastic-like composite resinous material that will adhere to tooth structure. When placed properly, it not only fills the cleaned-out cavity but literally restores it to almost its original natural structural integrity. This is in contrast to the mercury filling, which only sits in the tooth and will not adhere to it. If the interface between the mercury filling and the tooth structure is separated, bacteria will be able to enter and cause a cavity. This could eventually turn into a root canal procedure if the nerve is invaded.

The process of inserting the composite bonded filling has a steeper learning curve for dentists to master as compared with the mercury filling. It is a more detailed and time-consuming process. Layer upon layer of composite material is placed to fill the tooth. After each layer is packed into the tooth, the bonding light must be applied to harden it. The light only penetrates about a few millimeters deep. If the hole is greater than this, more layers must be applied incrementally, or the bonding light will not sufficiently harden the composite resin. This is a very attention-demanding process that provides a quality result. In my opinion, it is worth the extra time and detail, because there is no mercury involved. I will not change or lower the quality of my service for anything.

When Mr. Murray left my office, I thought about Expedodontics (notice that I am now using a capital E) and how I might be able to hasten the process of placing the fillings. Thinking about the bonded restoration, I quickly realized that I might be able to hasten its placement by thinking outside the box. Here was the issue. How could I place almost all the material needed, no matter how deep, in one step, and yet have the light penetrate as deeply as needed? The bonding light does not penetrate as effectively after about three to five millimeters deep. Its strength begins to attenuate with greater traveling distance. If the material is not completely cured, then it will irritate the tooth, causing pain. This seemed to be an enigmatic conundrum.

Then my epiphany occurred. What if I looked at this puzzle differently? What if I used another equally strong bonding material that did not require only the light to cure it? What if I had composite resin that set on its own, with or without the light? What if the depth of the cavity was not relevant, because it would still cure? I found that material, which was used to rebuild broken-down tooth structure for crowns to sit on. This was extremely strong material that set with or without the bonding light.

Not only did this technique provide a faster process, but I was able to contain costs for my patients with a more efficient service. Certainly, there is far more to this than what I am presently describing, but it worked exceedingly well.

Many years later, Lavanda, my chief clinical assistant, got a telephone call from a representative of a dental materials company. He wanted to provide us with a lunch-and-learn program. She agreed.

During this lovely luncheon, he explained how we would be able to perform fillings with a new material in one quick procedure. While he demonstrated this, Lavanda, Sade and my other clinical assistants looked at me and began to smile knowingly. After his program was concluded, Lavanda and Sade asked him what the cost would be for this "new" system. His reply was in the thousands of dollars. They then stated that if we bought his company's system we would have to raise our fees to accommodate this new procedure. Happily, he agreed and said that this was good for everyone. You should have seen the sour look on Lavanda's face as his words smashed into her ears. His response did not sit well with us.

I then told him how we had been doing the exact same thing with another material without any expensive equipment. We asked him how we could justify his equipment and material at greater cost, yet my system contained costs. His answer was for us to use his equipment for two weeks, at no cost to us, and see if we weren't happy.

Have you ever heard of the puppy dog sale? Someone in sales once told me about this. Here is how it works. The child sees the cute little puppy dog and pleads with the parent to have it. The mother says no, but the salesman invites them to take the puppy home for the weekend for free. If they still did not want the dog, then it could be returned a few days later. Knowing that most people will not return the dog, the salesman was comfortable providing this offer. That's how I viewed this salesman's pitch. Nonetheless, Lavanda agreed. She wanted to check out their system, but she felt totally comfortable telling him to take it back after two weeks.

It turned out to be a more complicated system than I had developed. We gave it back and still use our superior system.

Expedodontics. Thank you again, Mr. Murray.

24

JobSmiles™ and InvisiDent™

*"Without a sense of caring, there can be no sense of
community."*
—Anthony J. D'Angelo

*"Caring about others, running the risk of feeling, and
leaving an impact on people, brings happiness."*
—Rabbi Harold Kushner

P   *lease, you have to help me. I have been out of work for almost three years and am living*
at the poverty level.

I continued reading this letter, which certainly attracted my attention.

I can't get a job because of my teeth. Some are missing, and whatever are left are horrible to
look at. I cannot go to an interview. I'll be laughed at. Is there some way for you to help me so
that I can get back into the work force and resume a normal life? I have no money to pay you.
I am pleading with you.

I put down this letter on my desk and just gazed out the window, not really looking at anything but seeing much in my mind's eye. What events could have brought
someone to write a letter like this? How desperate she must be. I showed the letter
to my wife, who functions as my sounding board within my office.

"Clearly, you have to do something for this woman," Marji said to me.

"Okay. Let's call her and give her an appointment to find out what's going on here. I don't want to get involved with some crackpot or someone who just wants free dentistry for no good reason," I commented.

A few days later I met Miriam Calisto. As I walked down the hallway toward the treatment room, I could hear sobbing from within. She was seated in my dental chair with her head in her hands, and tears were running down her cheeks.

"Miriam, it's nice to meet you. Your letter sparked my interest. Would you please tell me your story?"

She turned to me and covered her mouth with her hand as she spoke. "With the downturn in the economy, I was let go. I have been unable to get the courage to interview in any company."

"Why is that?"

"My smile. I am disfigured and embarrassed to be seen in public."

"As a dentist, I see all types of smiles every day. Why don't you lower your hand, and let me see what you are talking about."

At first she was afraid to lower her hand, but then, ever so slowly, she lowered it. She did keep her lips closed.

"Come on. Let me see what all the fuss is about," I said rather curiously.

Then she gave me her idea of a smile.

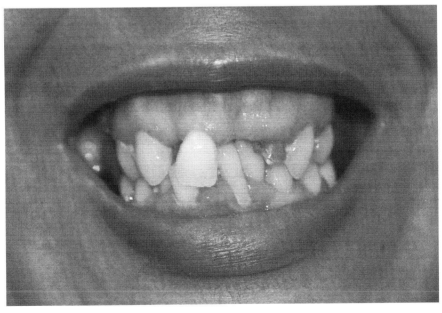

Miriam's smile before treatment

Instantly, I understood her problem. But I thought, *How can I help this woman?* Her condition was too involved for someone without the means of affording dental care. My wife had mentioned our desire to give back to the community in a more meaningful gesture than all of the other activities we participate in. Suddenly, it all became clear to me. There must be many people, out of work, too embarrassed to seek interviews because of their teeth. What if I started a charity called JobSmiles™, designed to help people get back into the work force? But how could I do this and not go broke in the process? Then I thought about the explosions in Germany.

For years dentists had the ability to make partial dentures with metal clasping. I'm sure that you have seen these dental appliances. They have those unsightly hooks around the teeth to hold the denture in place. Sometimes the sparkle of metal brings unwanted attention to their presence in the mouth. Challenges always bring on solutions. Using a special nylon-based plastic, a more cosmetic partial denture was devised to solve this condition. The material was pink and without metal. It blended into the gum line, providing a cosmetic result. This seemed like the cure for partially missing teeth without heavy metal. But as is always the case, it was not without its limitations.

This nylon-based material would not allow adding additional teeth to it if another tooth had to be extracted. If a nylon clasp broke, it could not be repaired easily. A new partial denture would have to be made, adding on additional cost. It also had a thickness that patients found annoying. But that was all that existed, and people got used to it. Then the fires started.

It turns out that the nylon used to make this type of denture was produced in a factory in Germany. A fire caused its production to be halted. The demand for a cosmetic partial denture still existed, even though there was now a scarcity of nylon. Then a plastic manufacturer in the United States created a similar material without nylon. Strangely enough, this new material was an improvement over the nylon-based material. I had started to use it and soon discovered that it was superior to the nylon.

It was thinner and more lightweight, creating greater comfort. Its gum-colored clasps blended more aesthetically than the nylon. But the greatest improvement was its ability to be repaired easily. Additional teeth could be added to it without having to make another denture. This would keep costs down. I thought about Miriam.

What if I could give her a beautiful smile without extensive treatment? What if I could return her self-confidence? And what if I provided this to her absolutely free because of her present economical circumstance?

I offered this to Miriam, and she replied with big hugs laced with tears of joy. When we finished her treatment, she looked at herself in the mirror, not believing her transformation, and through continued tears of joy asked, "What do you call this?"

I thought about it and then answered rather directly, "InvisiDent™. That's what I'll call it."

Now I had virtually invisible partial dentures to offer the patient. The new name was perfect for this. When a patient asks us for replacement teeth that can keep costs down while producing a cosmetic result, we respond, "InvisiDent." I love it.

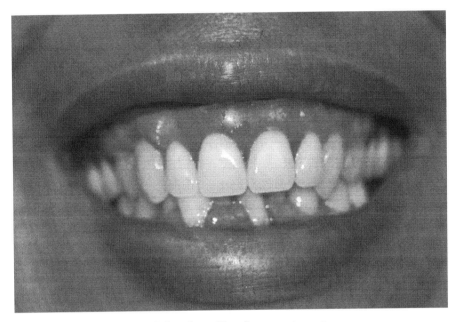

Miriam's smile after treatment

Do you think she was happy? I know, it's a silly question. The good part was that my entire staff was thrilled for her. Everyone felt good. That's the power of giving. So my wife looked at me and said, "Where do we go from here?"

"Why not start a small charitable movement called JobSmiles™?" I replied. "This will help those less fortunate to get back into the work force when their poor smiles intimidate them."

Everyone agreed. My wife has been charged with creating our 501(c)(3) foundation called JobSmiles™. In the meantime, we provide this act of giving to those who have every good reason to need it. Now, that's something to smile about.

DENTAL TIP:

When you've lost your crown

No, I'm not advocating the overthrow of the king. This relates to the loss of your dental crown. Should it fall out—and it always occurs after hours, when the office is closed—simply go to the drugstore and buy a denture adhesive. Fixodent, Polident, or any other sticky denture adhesive will do. Scratching the existing cement inside the crown with the sharp point of a safety pin helps to remove some of this material. It will be very hard and difficult to do. Try your best. Wash it, reseat the crown without the denture adhesive, and check your bite. If all seems comfortable, then remove it and reseat it with some of the adhesive. Close your teeth to push down the crown properly. If your bite is off, remove it and start all over again. Wipe off the excess adhesive and wait thirty minutes before eating. Then call the office to schedule an appointment for a permanent cementation. I don't know why, but after almost forty years of clinical practice I have found this tends to happen before weddings, christenings, bar mitzvahs, or vacations. There must be some sort of gremlin who rules these events. I know it's not the tooth fairy.

25

RABBIS BLESS POPE IN THE VATICAN

Now, that is a title for a chapter! It grabs the reader's attention and curiosity. How could such an event occur?

Okay, so at this point, we have become acquainted with each other. You know me, and if you have gotten this far in my book, then I know you. You are obviously a highly intelligent curious individual looking to help yourself or someone you love. You enjoy the search for knowledge and its application.

I would like to take this time to share an amazing story with you, which has absolutely nothing whatsoever to do with dentistry. It is, however, one of the most amazing true stories you will ever read. I know, because I was there. What follows next is an article I wrote, which was published in a number of newspapers in 2005. It is about an experience of a lifetime. I would like to share it with you. I believe you'll enjoy it. This article is presented exactly the way it was published. Enjoy.

RABBIS BLESS POPE IN THE VATICAN
An Eyewitness Account in the Vatican
By
Harvey Passes, D.D.S.

I am a dentist who practices in Great Neck, New York. I have just had the experience of a lifetime. Dreams are rarely this good. Imagine being in the Apostolic Palace in the Vatican where there is a worldwide delegation of Jews seated with the expectation of a private audience with His Holiness John Paul II. It is to be a meeting of gratitude within the tone of reconciliation.

The marble floors of the palace stretch to highly polished ancient wood and marble walls, which climb at least 40 feet. About halfway up, these walls are adorned with the most incredible frescoes created some 500 years ago perhaps by the likes of Michelangelo, Raphael or other legendary artists. The sheer size of the artistry boggles the mind. I am sitting in the front row with my childhood friend Gary Krupp. I never would have imagined that such an event would take place with my participation. My friend is making good on a dream, his dream of peace on earth and goodwill to all men. This is a story that spans 800 years in the making. It would read like a novel except that it is true. It all happened.

Some years ago my friend Gary performed some special favors for the Vatican. A hospital was being built in Italy. Difficulties occurred and he was asked to assist. He did so unselfishly. Gary wouldn't accept any payment for his services. Sometime later he was asked again to assist with more problem solving. Again, he refused payment. The Pope was so impressed with this Jewish gentleman's unselfish philanthropic behavior that he bestowed upon him the title of Knight of Saint Gregory the Great. He is the seventh Jewish person ever given this honor by a pope. What happened next intensifies my story.

Sometime later Gary found himself at a benefit dinner where some rabbis were discussing the desire of Jewish scholars to see the Maimonides papers. These papers reflect the writings of Maimonides, a Jewish philosopher, rabbi and physician who lived during the 12th century. These documents have been in the Vatican library for centuries and Jewish scholars have been denied access to them. During this benefit dinner one of the rabbis wondered if they would ever be able to see them. Someone told them to speak to Gary. The rabbis looked at this person wondering if this was a joke or was he serious. They approached Gary and he said he would look into it. They did not know that Gary was now a member of the Papal household. Weeks later Gary called the rabbis stating that the Vatican had agreed to this momentous request. A trip to Rome allowed the eyes of Jewish scholars to view these sacred manuscripts from the ancient sage. The Vatican greeted this august assembly with much warmth and generosity. Upon returning home many celebratory events were held to honor Gary's accomplishment. Then I got the phone call.

Gary said that he wanted to "devote his life to peace among religions, especially the Middle East." How does one react to this kind of a statement? You may as well attempt to move the ocean across the street with a spoon. Gary was firm, sure of himself and aggressively ambitious in this pursuit. He felt that attaining his title from the Pope was more than happenstance. With the respect of the Jewish people and now the Roman Catholic Church, he would have the ability to accomplish much. *Pave the Way Foundation* is the result of this desire. It is an organization that is "paving the way" for peace in various regions of the world. This is a not-for-profit foundation working to reach various worldwide religious and governmental levels of support. Gary asked me to be on his Board of Directors. It seemed a natural thing to do as we have been friends since the age of 16 and have always respected each other's opinion. What happened next astounded me.

Pave the Way Foundation began to shuttle between New York, Rome and Jerusalem with stops along the way to England and other cities. Relationships began building between *Pave the Way Foundation* and various ambassadors to the United Nations, cardinals, bishops, Israeli and Palestinian officials and more. The Foundation was able to negotiate the amazing loan of the Maimonides papers to Israel as a gesture of goodwill from the Vatican. This is all being done through *Pave the Way Foundation*. Much can be accomplished through the "gesture of goodwill." Just when I thought things could not realistically get any better, Gary announces that "*Pave the Way Foundation* has been granted a private audience with His Holiness John Paul II."

During a Board of Directors meeting Gary let it be known that he had been working on a meeting of gratitude and thanks to His Holiness for his defense of Jews before his papacy as well as during it. Under his pontificate the Vatican recognized the State of Israel by exchanging ambassadors. Pope John Paul II was the first Pope since Saint Peter to visit a synagogue. He also visited the Western Wall in Jerusalem and left an inscribed message within the wall asking for forgiveness. He has also made it a sin to be anti-Semitic. He has been a friend to the Jewish people and has tried to bridge the ancient gap. *Pave the Way Foundation* would bring a worldwide delegation of 100 rabbis, 12 cantors and Jewish leaders to offer prayers of thanks and gratitude to His Holiness. The pope happily agreed to this request.

On January 18th at 11:30 am we all assembled within the Vatican's Apostolic Palace to meet Pope John Paul II. Our speech was presented first, by Gary Krupp, as follows:

"Your Holiness:

We are a group of people who represent a cross section of Judaism, who have traveled here with the blessings of millions of our faith in order to thank you.

Soon after your ascension to the throne of St. Peter, you made a telling trip to Auschwitz in order to pay homage to victims of the Holocaust. You have defended the Jewish people at every opportunity, as a priest in Poland and during your twenty-six year pontificate. You have denounced anti-Semitism as a "sin against God and humanity." This tone of reconciliation has been the corner stone of your papacy and its relations with the Jewish people.

On April 13, 1986, you became the first Pope since St. Peter to visit a synagogue. Upon presenting his credentials to you in June 2003, Israeli Ambassador Oded Ben-Hur expressed this enormous gesture best when he said, "On that day you took upon your shoulders the 2000 year old church, back to the first century synagogue of Capernaum, where Jesus used to pray, thus closing an historic circle."

You moved the Holy See to initiate the process of normalizing diplomatic relations with the state of Israel in 1992, the beloved biblical homeland of the Jewish people, symbolically acknowledging the existence of Eretz Yisrael yesterday, today, and forever.

Your pilgrimage to Israel and the Holy Land on March 21, 2000, was immortalized in the hearts and minds of the Jewish people around the world, when you placed your prayer asking for forgiveness in the Western Wall.

Your solemn remarks during your visit to the Hall of Remembrance, Yad Vashem profoundly moved us and touched our hearts.

It is impossible to describe the emotional impact these milestones have had on Jews worldwide. Your Holiness, these reconciliatory acts have, in fact, been a hallmark of your pontificate as you have also tried to repair the ancient rifts in all of the religions in the world. The Jewish Ethics of the Fathers beautifully captures, in verse, the love you have exhibited for all humanity. Rabbi Hillel says: "Be among the disciples of Aaron, by being a lover of peace, a pursuer of peace, a lover of all humanity and bringing them closer to religion".

For your acts of love of all humankind and your implacable pursuit of peace and reconciliation of all the faiths, your Holiness truly is the personification of these ideals and spirit of Aaron, the high priest of ancient Israel.

In closing, you have referred to us, the children of Abraham, as your beloved elder brothers. My prayerful wish is that Jews, Christians and Muslims, the three children of Abraham, may soon bond together in one common cause and voice to defend all humanity against those who defame God by committing wanton acts of violence in his holy name.

Your Holiness, Thank you, thank you, thank you. Shalom, Shalom, Shalom."

As a thunderous applause erupted from the audience I could see that Pope John Paul II was visibly moved. He applauded and smiled. He looked at each and every one of us. A feeling of love and brotherhood flowed throughout the room. Then he responded.

"Dear Friends,

With affection I greet the members of the *"Pave the Way Foundation"* on your visit to the Vatican, and I thank Mr. Krupp for the kind words which he has addressed to me on your behalf. This year we will be celebrating the fortieth anniversary of the Second Vatican Council's Declaration Nostra Aetate, which has significantly contributed to the strengthening of Jewish-Catholic dialogue. May this be an occasion for renewed commitment to increased understanding and cooperation in the service of building a world ever more firmly based on respect for the divine image in every human being.

Upon all of you, I invoke the abundant blessings of the Almighty and, in particular, the gift of peace. Shalom Aleichem."

From right, Gary & Merry Krupp and me listening to the Pope.

More joyful thunderous applause filled the room. Most people in the great hall were aware of the Second Vatican Council's Declaration Nostra Aetate which stated that Jews were not collectively responsible for the death of Christ and that "...in her rejection of every persecution against any man, the Church, mindful of the patrimony she shares with the Jews and moved not by political reasons but by the Gospel's spiritual love, decries hatred, persecutions, displays of anti-Semitism, directed against Jews at any time and by anyone."

Then I and a few members of the Board of Directors got up to present the pope a gift. It was a glass sculpture of two open palm hands holding the globe. It signified a humanitarian award to the pope. He graciously accepted it. Three rabbis stood up and approached him. They spoke a prayer and blessed him. This was the first time that anyone in the Vatican could remember the pope being blessed and not the other way around. He then blessed our congregation. Twelve cantors began to sing songs of prayer filling the room with optimism and hope. The pope physically extended his hand to members of *Pave the Way Foundation.* One by one we shook his hand as we looked into each other's eyes. Then something wonderful happened.

My momentous handshake with His Holiness

Pope John Paul II asked the entire congregation to step forward so that he could shake their hands as well. Members of the papal household started to hand out gifts to all of us. His Holiness was in a very good mood and wanted to share this feeling with all of us. It was then that I remembered the *Pave the Way Foundation* slogan, **EMBRACE OUR SIMILARITIES, SAVOR OUR DIFFERENCES**.

What an experience. This is a journey worth taking.
Shalom. Pax. Salome Aleikem. Peace be with you.

Whether it is within the dental office or life's stage, tolerance and effective communication hold the key to unlocking the door of well-meaning understanding. What could be better than the gift of giving love and mutual respect? What more can I say?

26

BEING LONG IN THE TOOTH

"Growing old is like being increasingly penalized for a crime
you haven't committed."
—ANONYMOUS

In the album *Bookends* by Simon and Garfunkel, they recorded some elderly people making comments on aging. One particularly memorable statement from an older gentleman was, "I have no choice. I have to be an old man." With luck and a proper lifestyle, we should all be able to say that. The problem is remaining physically and mentally healthy.

"My wife complains about the sound my upper denture makes when I eat," stated Abe Stark rather indignantly. "I couldn't care less about the sound. My denture feels fine. I'm only here because she is getting on my nerves about this."

"Abe, how old are you?" I asked.

"Ninety-two and I feel great. I'm president of my homeowners association and live a very active life."

Looking at Abe I could see that to be a fact. A tall man with the look of authority adorned by a full mane of thick white hair, Abe's appearance was manicured and polished. By no means would anyone take him for ninety-two. Frankly, over the past fifteen years, I have been observing more and more people in their eighties and upward visiting my office and sharing tales of tennis, business, travel, and more. We are living longer and acting as if we are twenty years younger. Sixty is the new forty, while eighty is the new sixty, and on and on. It's very impressive.

"I don't want to spend anything on a new denture. I've had this one between five or ten years. It fits fine. I do not earn an income. I'm here just because of my wife," Abe continued with an air of defiant authority. He obviously was used to getting what he wanted, except when it concerned his wife.

"Can I look at your denture?"

"Of course."

He removed and handed it to me. On close examination, I saw that it was fine and would just need a reline.

A denture reline is the process of flowing some pink denture plastic inside it to conform to the upper or lower jaw. As we age, the jawbone begins to shrink. The denture stays the same as it was the day it was made. A small void is created, contributing to the denture's movement in the mouth during eating or speaking.

Already knowing the truth, I asked anyway, "When was last time you had this denture relined?"

"It was never relined."

"I have good news for you. You will not need a new denture. This just needs to be relined. It is an economical and easy one-visit procedure. You will also save money, since you won't need a new denture."

"I don't really care, but if it will get my wife off my back, I'll do it," continued Abe.

We were able to perform this for him right away. After it was completed he was impressed at how comfortably snug it felt. He confessed that he had a greater feeling of confidence in opening his mouth and talking due to its improved stability.

"You should thank your wife for advising you to do this," I said.

As only a great sage of ninety-two years could state Abe replied, "Women! Can't live with them. Can't live without them."

I half smiled as I soaked in this immense philosophical epiphany.

27

SPECIAL NEEDS OF THE ELDERLY

"You can't help getting older, but you don't have to get old."
—GEORGE BURNS

Just as children have special needs so do the elderly. Our bodies change, especially as we age. Never before have so many people experienced older age than we are seeing today. This brings with it new challenges. Here is some information you should be aware of for yourself or a loved one fortunate to be living longer.

It is not true that as we age, we can expect to develop tooth loss, dry mouth, or toothaches. These conditions are by-products of gum disease, tooth decay, or side-effects of medications. It's simple—by maintaining good preventive oral-health care, you should be able to minimize dental conditions from occurring. But sometimes as we age, depression sets in, which prevents us from performing the proper behavior that is in our best interest.

What follows is a brief list of circumstances influencing the dental condition of the elderly. Once understood, it can be managed.

- *Lack of dental insurance or funds needed to afford proper dental care.* My staff always asks a simple yet fundamental question, "What can we do to help you afford your dental treatment?" When the economy collapsed in 2008, we decided to create our own affordable dental plan. This opened the door to those without dental insurance and allowed them to maintain good dental care.

- *Inability to get to dental offices.* Some elderly people can no longer drive and public transportation can be too complicated. In some circumstances we have been able to provide a car service to those in need, so they can have their dentistry completed.
- *Side effects of medications.* The elderly are known for consuming great quantities of medications. We use a computerized reference library that compares the patient's medications with what is customarily given in the dental office. We also review side effects and advise the patient on how to reduce deleterious effects on teeth. Dry mouth is a very common complaint. There are some over-the-counter products that can be used to assist with this condition.
- *Recurring decay around old fillings and on the gum line where the gums have receded.* As we age, many of us lose our bone and gum tissue around our teeth. This exposes the root surface. This region is very soft and becomes decayed quite easily. If there are old fillings in this area, then their margins become decayed easily as well. In-office fluoride applications followed up with home fluoride treatments helps to prevent this from happening in most cases. Failing fillings need to be replaced. More holistic bonded fillings are advisable.
- *Gum disease and oral cancer.* Every checkup visit should include an oral cancer screening as well as a periodontal (gum and bone) evaluation. As we age, our immune system becomes compromised. A lifetime of smoking, drinking, and poor oral-health care contributes heavily to the onset of these notorious conditions. The hygienist uses advanced chemiluminescent light technology to help detect oral abnormalities including oral cancer screening. This innovative high-tech procedure shows suspicious areas in the mouth very clearly. In fact, it can highlight lesions sometimes not observed with the naked eye. When detected early, oral cancer is one of the easiest malignancies to cure.
- *Poor diet and a lack of appreciation for good oral health.* It's no secret that the elderly can sometimes forget about performing effective hygiene habits. The mouth is a prime source for this neglect. It is critical that these people not forget their personal health maintenance obligations. A simple note taped to the bathroom mirror stating BRUSH YOUR TEETH sometimes is all that is needed. Teeth should be brushed for two minutes at least two times per day with fluoride-based toothpaste. To help with diminished hand dexterity, it is advised to use an electric toothbrush. Flossing by hand or with one of the new floss devices is excellent. This can be followed up with an oral-irrigation appliance such as a Waterpik. After meals, sugar-free gum should be chewed for twenty minutes. This process stimulates the flow of saliva, which remineralizes the enamel of the teeth, helping to resist decay. Drink copious amounts of water to keep the body hydrated and the flow of saliva constant, which will remineralize teeth.

Closing this chapter with some interesting quotes on aging from sages of the past piqued my fancy. Enjoy.

"Age is an issue of mind over matter. If you don't mind, it doesn't matter."
—MARK TWAIN

"As I grow older, I pay less attention to what men say. I just watch what they do."
—ANDREW CARNEGIE

"Nobody grows old merely by living a number of years. We grow old by deserting our ideals. Years may wrinkle the skin, but to give up enthusiasm wrinkles the soul."
—SAMUEL ULLMAN

"A diplomat is a man who always remembers a woman's birthday but never remembers her age."
—ROBERT FROST

"Old age is no place for sissies."
—BETTE DAVIS

"I will never be an old man. To me, old age is always fifteen years older than I am."
—FRANCIS BACON

"An archaeologist is the best husband a woman can have. The older she gets, the more interested he is in her."
—AGATHA CHRISTIE

28

A THIRD SET OF TEETH?

"I invent nothing. I rediscover."
—AUGUSTE RODIN

With a look of astonished perplexity, Sanjay asked, "What do you mean, a third set of teeth?"

"Today it's not as mysterious as it used to be," I said to my new patient. He was missing all of his teeth and inquired about having them replaced with something fixed in his mouth. He was not happy with his dentures. They moved around a lot during eating and talking.

"May I tell you a story?"

"Sure."

I began this story in 1967. At that time, if a patient wanted to replace missing teeth with implants, it would have to be done with either a blade or a transosteal implant. These metal implants relied on being mechanically held within or on the jawbone. They did not fuse with the bone. The dental profession looked upon this procedure with some degree of skepticism.

In 1952, however, a serendipitous event occurred in Sweden. A research orthopedist, Per-Ingvar Brånemark, discovered something completely unexpected. He noticed that after inserting a titanium screw within the bone of a rabbit he could not remove it. This revolutionized dentistry. It revealed a natural secret: bone can integrate with titanium. This led Brånemark to develop root-shaped titanium implants to be used on humans. It took him at least fifteen years to prove that the biological fusion of bone to metal could indeed be done. He coined the phrase osseointegration. Today this miracle of dental science is a most common practice with a high degree of success.

After hearing this story Sanjay asked, "So how could this help me with my dentures?"

"The miracle of dental implants presents you with options never seen before. For the first time, you can have all of your teeth replaced with another set of teeth. These teeth could be fixed into your mouth, functioning just as your real ones did. Or, you could keep your existing dentures and anchor them to a few implants. I would place some metal snaps, almost like the kind you have on your shirt. Notice that each has a male and female part. The two pieces snap together. A similar concept exists for implants. One piece goes into the implant, and the other goes in the underside of your denture. It just snaps into place, allowing you the pleasure of chewing anything your heart desires."

"Amazing! There are so many things waiting to be discovered," marveled Sanjay. "But explain the process. Is it painful? How long does it take?"

"You would be completely numb and not feel a thing. Also, most people are not aware that their bone does not have any nerves in them. You couldn't feel any pain anyway. The procedure is relatively quick. We place them right here in my office. Depending upon where they are placed, the osseointegration could take anywhere from three to six months. Would you like us to begin the process of learning if you are a candidate for implants?"

"Yes. When can we begin?"

"Right now."

To see an animation on how this works, please visit my Web site at http://www.passesdentalcare.com/treatment/dental-implants.aspx.

Dental implants are truly one of man's great medical marvels.

29

AT YOUR SERVICE

*"One never stands so tall as when they stoop
to help another."*
—ANONYMOUS

By this time, you have already noticed that when I first meet them, I ask my patients, "How may I serve you?" Many people have asked me why I always say that. Some feel that I am placing myself in a subservient position. The truth is that this is not true. It is the way I view my role in society.

After forty years of clinical practice, I discovered that I am a caregiver. I thoroughly enjoy helping, supporting, and yes, servicing others. Contrary to being subservient, I feel that I am in a noble position. My quote above is precisely the way I feel. This attitude pervades my practice. I will only hire people who feel the same. You cannot teach someone to feel this way. Either you have it, or you don't. As I have mentioned previously, the purpose of life is a life full of purpose. My purpose has always been to help others. Giving is a self-enriching feeling.

So when I ask, "How may I serve you?" I am opening doors, breaking down barriers, allowing people to become more comfortable with me and my staff. Let's see if Betty agrees.

"I work at North Shore Hospital. Gloria Torres works in the office next door to mine. Last week I saw her smile for the first time and was surprised at how pretty she looked. I noticed that something was different about Gloria but didn't know what it was. She looked younger. When I asked her she told me that she had her old broken-down bridgework replaced by you. She said that for years she had been too embarrassed to smile because of it. Now she feels more confident in the way she looks," said Betty Fairfield.

Betty was on a roll, so I just shook my head in understanding and kept quiet while she took front stage, revealing her inner feelings.

"I've been so self-conscious about my smile. For years I gave to everyone else in my family. I always came last. Now I'm seventy-one years old, and the people I've cared for are either taking care of their families, or they're dead." Then with an almost defiant yet triumphant decision she stated, "It's time for me to take care of myself."

Somehow I felt that I didn't have to be in the room for her to say what she had just confessed. It was as if a sudden realization had just taken hold of her, and she'd blurted it out loud so that she could hear it from herself. I smiled and asked her my famous question, "How can I serve you?"

"I want beautiful teeth. I want to smile to the world. I'm a good person, but people think I'm sad or even mad because I never smile. I want you to give me a beautiful smile," Betty said with a quickening pace as she listened to herself speak.

"All right. But first, I must tell you how grateful I am that you selected my office to come to. There are many others you could have gone to but didn't. When I present to you the various options available to you, I need you to be able to do three things for yourself. You must see if what I say feels right professionally, then personally, and finally spiritually. In your heart of hearts you must feel that it is right for you. You need to realize a sense of joy and hopefulness in your decision. And finally, my staff must figure out a way to make it affordable for you in order to achieve your dream."

Her mouth just dropped at hearing this. "No doctor ever spoke to me like this. I think I'm going to be happy here. When can we start?" Betty said with an expression of joy and hope.

As I have said to my children countless times, nothing feels better than when you help others and see them smile.

Dental Tip:

The Ultimate Tooth and Gum Care Program

Want to wake up without bad breath? Want cleaner teeth? Want to kill bacteria in your mouth? Try this for the absolute best maintenance of your teeth and gums. It's real simple but will take a little more time than what you are presently doing. The payoff for you will be that you should have lower dental repair costs. And, who knows, you might just keep your teeth for your lifetime. Follow this step by step process below:

1. *Floss all of your teeth with Glide floss.*
2. *Brush your teeth with a Sonicare or Rotadent electronic toothbrush thirty seconds for each quadrant of your mouth. Use any American Dental Association (ADA) approved toothpaste.*
3. *Rinse the toothpaste with salt water.*
4. *In a shot glass, place a small amount of baking soda and add a few drops of hydrogen peroxide until you have the consistency of freshly fallen snow.*
   a. *Take a rubber oral stimulator and place some of this mixture on your finger and wipe it in the area where your gums meet your teeth. Gently pump the oral stimulator between the teeth or move it in a circular fashion for ten times between each of your teeth from the cheek side and then the inside.*
   b. *With the remaining mixture place it on the toothbrush and brush your teeth with it.*
5. *Finally, rinse your mouth with an ADA approved daily fluoride mouth rinse before going to bed.*
6. *Do this before bedtime and awaken with neutral breath odor.*

Here's how it works. Aside from removing your mealtime residue about your teeth you'll be killing the bacteria with the baking soda and hydrogen peroxide. The salt water also helps to destroy the bacteria by bursting their cell walls. The oral stimulator builds stronger gums by initiating the increased production of keratin within your gum tissue. This is the same material on the soles of your feet and your elbows. The electronic tooth brush is far more efficient than what you can do manually with the old fashioned toothbrush. The fluoride continues to strengthen your enamel.

This is one dental tip that you will thank me for over and over again.

30

MY DREAM COMES TRUE

"I must say I find television very educational.
The minute somebody turns it on, I go to the
library and read a good book."
—GROUCHO MARX

With what was becoming a habitual question of incredulity I asked, "Is this a joke?" It all started with my development of the Holmium: YAG laser for dentistry.

Around 1989, I purchased my first dental laser. Its various uses sparked my fascination with this amazing technology. As is my nature, I jumped in headfirst with a few other dentists across America and cofounded the Academy of Laser Dentistry. This august organization became the world's most recognized source of information, education, professional training, and proficiency testing for lasers in dentistry. In New York, I had catapulted to its most noted spokesman. Newspapers, radio stations, and television shows were requesting interviews with me as new lasers were being developed. It was great fun. Then, my world changed.

"Could you perform a demonstration with the dental laser being used on a patient?" asked a producer from Long Island's Cablevision.

"Sure," I replied. "How would you like to see a smile makeover using a laser?"

"Great. What's involved?" the Cablevision producer said.

And so it went until he brightened my day by setting up a date for this to be broadcast live all morning on *News 12 Long Island*. When the day came, my staff was all aflutter for this three-hour live television shoot. It went very well. Many people called, expressing delight at seeing us on television. All in all it was a very exciting day. At the end of the day, someone called me with an invitation to do another television shoot.

"I watched you on *News 12* this morning and found you to be quite entertaining as well as informative. How would you like to appear on my show?" said the voice on the phone.

"What show is that?" I queried.

"*The Jewish Entertainment Hour on Telecare.*" This is a Catholic channel owned by the Archdiocese of Rockville Center Long Island. A better incongruity you will never find.

"Is this a joke?" I asked while checking to see if the date was April first.

"No, I assure you that this is not a joke. Can you sing or tell jokes?"

This was getting better all the time. "Yes, I can do both. If I sing, then I'll bring my guitar to your studio."

"Fantastic. You could also discuss the dental laser."

What was I getting myself into? was my initial thought. He titled my interview "The Singing Dentist," and it was seen by many people. It was received warmly.

Then it got crazier. "We just saw you on the *Jewish Entertainment Hour* and would like to interview you for the Sunday *New York Times*," the new caller said.

I responded with what was becoming a habitual reply. "Is this a joke?"

"No, I assure you that we are interested in the Singing Dentist. We would like to focus on your singing to your patients and shoot some photos of them in your office as you treat them."

Going along on this loony-tunes ride, I accepted and selected a date for them to visit my office.

After this interview and its publication, I received another wacky phone call from Cablevision's *News 12* again.

"Dr. Passes, a new dental laser has just been developed, and we'd like to interview you in the studio on it. Would you be willing to come down for this?"

"Of course. This would be a great way to let the public know about its features and benefits." We picked a date, and I hung up.

The next day I got another phone call from Cablevision *News 12* asking me to perform as the Singing Dentist in my office. "We saw your article in the *New York Times* and felt that it would be a great human interest story."

I was gratified and accepted this invitation. "Fancy that," I said out loud to no one in my office. "*News 12* twice in one week."

The zaniest call came a few hours later. It was from the director of *News 12*. "Dr. Passes?"

"Yes. How can I serve you?" I replied.

"I just reviewed our schedule and recognized that you will be interviewed twice in the same week."

"Yes?"

"I'm sorry but I cannot have you in the news twice in the same week. It will look like you paid us for your public relations."

"That's okay," I said. "I understand. I guess we'll drop the Singing Dentist piece and work with the new laser. I'm really excited about telling the public about it because of its…"

"Dr. Passes, I'm sorry to interrupt you but you will not be doing the piece on the laser. We want the Singing Dentist."

Talk about shock and awe. "But that's fluff. It has no substance," I said, not believing the turn this was taking.

"*News 12* concerns itself with human-interest stories. It's the Singing Dentist or nothing."

"I'm tuning up my guitar," I responded rather forlornly.

The news crew came down to my office and broadcasted the Singing Dentist for all of Long Island to enjoy. But that's not the end of this story. What happened next completely changed my life and experience.

"Dr. Passes?" the caller said. "I'm from Long Island Cablevision."

"How nice. How can I serve you?" I answered rather curiously. This was beginning to become a pattern.

"We have been watching you and would like to offer you your own television show if we are satisfied with your pilot."

"Is this a joke?" was all I could say.

"I assure you that this is not a joke. We'd like to meet with you to discuss this."

And so it went. I nervously accepted this offer and met with them. *What am I getting myself into?* was my constant thought.

"We will take care of everything behind the camera. You are responsible for what's in front of the camera. In other words the show's content, its guests, and any graphic rendering. You create, we produce," said the Cablevision lady.

And so it went. I came up with my first show. I waited three weeks for their decision. Would they accept it or would my chance at local stardom be doomed and brushed into the dustbin of the has-beens?

The call came with acceptance and a genuine feeling that my show would be successful. This has been one of the most amazing experiences of my life. On the job I learned how to produce and host a television interview show. Originally the show was called *Tooth or Consequences.* As you might imagine it was all about dentistry. Dentists from all over North America came to be interviewed. Eventually, I expanded my horizon to include physicians, lawyers, politicians, wine makers, local businesspeople, teachers, singers, magicians, actors, and so many more. My favorite people to interview are authors. The passion they feel for their subject is unsurpassed by any other group. Their research is excellent, providing a wonderful show full of great content. Barnes & Noble developed a relationship with me. They provided me with authors to interview. I am especially partial to Long Island writers. Cablevision suggested that I change the name to *Dr. Passes Presents*, since I was no longer dealing exclusively with dentistry. I agreed and was delighted to see my name in *TV Guide*. The show ultimately was broadcasted eight times a week. At last count I have produced and hosted 506 thirty-minute television shows.

An unexpected result of this show was my becoming an on camera consultant for NBC's *Today Show*, Fox's *Good Day New York*, WPIX *Morning News*, CBS *Evening News*, 1010 WINS, *News 12 Long Island*, and many more media outlets.

This experience taught me how to comport myself in front of thousands of eyes. There was no way I could have learned how to speak and listen in a more effective and meaningful manner. I am grateful to Cablevision for granting me this most unusual opportunity.

Thank you, Cablevision.

31

HELLENIC ORAL HEALTH CARE

"I told my dentist my teeth are going yellow.
He told me to wear a brown tie."
—RODNEY DANGERFIELD

Want a little bit of paradise, close by? If you take the Long Island Expressway east to Riverhead, you could get off at exit 71 and make a left onto Edwards Avenue. Travel northerly four miles until Sound Avenue. There, you turn right for about twenty-six vineyard-filled miles.

If you have never gone there, you are in for a true treat. It is something totally unexpected especially if you have lived in New York your entire life. It feels like another part of the country. In East Marion, you will come upon a restaurant called the Hellenic. The experience is unique. As usual, I'm getting ahead of myself.

Some years back, my family and I went there for dinner and met the Greek family who owns this venerable establishment. George Giannaris, restaurateur, chef, and son of its founder, met us, and our families have become, well, like family with each other. George is a true Renaissance man—an observant, highly intelligent, generous, gracious human being. He is also an amazingly talented innovative chef.

One day George related this story of frustration. "This gentleman comes into my restaurant impeccably dressed. His clothes, hair, and demeanor were very distinguished and well kept. Then he opens his mouth to speak, displaying only a few yellow teeth. The holes in his smile completely extinguished his dapper appearance.

It was shocking to see," George said with an incredulous expression on his face. He spoke this way because he is also an author. "Why doesn't he take care of his teeth?"

I just smiled and said, "Welcome to my world."

Before I could continue, George said, "He must have infections and layers of tartar in his mouth. I know that this supports the bacteria in your mouth to produce toxins that spread throughout your body. Frankly, it's disgusting. All he has to do is brush his teeth and get a checkup twice a year."

What a joy for me to hear someone talk about preventive dental care. It's truly rare for me to communicate with someone other than a dentist on the merits of routine oral healthcare. I am now in the process of trying to convince George to put floss and after-dinner mints on all of his tables.

Okay, so the floss might not be such a great idea after a romantic dinner. But hey, you never know.

32

CATCH THE BUZZ

*"One who gains strength by overcoming obstacles possesses
the only strength which can overcome adversity."*
— ALBERT SCHWEITZER
"True success is overcoming the fear of being unsuccessful."
— PAUL SWEENEY

One day Daniel DuBois comes to my office for routine care and he notices Tiffany wearing a pewter bumblebee pin on her lapel. Then he sees that Meena and all of the other staff are wearing the same thing. As his curiosity builds he asked the question, "What's with the bumblebees?"

Tiffany proudly replies, "According to the laws of aerodynamics, which governs the principles on how airplanes fly, the bumblebee should not be able to fly. Its wings are too small for its much larger oval body. The bumblebee was designed without the proper aerodynamic proportion."

Always the intelligent observer, Daniel was becoming locked into his deeper interest while continuing his question with, "So, what's with the bumblebees?"

Listening intently to this expected line of questioning Meena jumped in with, "It's like this. Conventional wisdom states that it's impossible for it to fly. Yet, it does fly. The problem is that no one ever told the bumblebee that it could not fly. We feel the same way."

As the dawn of recognition appeared on his face, Daniel started to respond when Tiffany took back the conversation with, "You see we believe that there isn't anything we can't do. We ignore people telling us it can't be done. We feel that we'll meet all challenges. Our goal is to help our patients in any way we can. We will not listen to *it can't be done.*"

"So, what you are saying is that the bumblebee pin is a reminder and a statement of your desire to meet challenges," Daniel added.

"Yes it is," Meena now chimed in. "But there's more. We are starting a blog and a newsletter on this idea for our patients."

"What do you mean?" asked Daniel.

"We want others to catch our feeling on never giving up. So, on a routine basis we'll write a column called *Catch the Buzz*, which will describe some of our stories. But more importantly we want to retell stories of perseverance from our patients. We want our patients to share with us their challenges and how they overcame adversity to become successful in their quest. When we publish their story we'll give them a pewter bumblebee to wear proudly as they repeat their story to others," Meena continued.

Catching the buzz Daniel suddenly became passionate in his next statement, "You know, I deserve a bumblebee. For the past ten years I have walked out of numerous dental offices because of my dental fear. This is the first dental office where I have finally broken this fear and have successfully completed two root canal procedures, received posts and crowns and finally underwent a complete smile makeover. Doesn't that deserve a bumblebee?" he asked rather proudly.

I had walked into the room somewhere in the middle of this conversation and had decided to add my own two cents with, "Daniel, there is absolutely no discussion on your deserving the bumblebee pin. You have proved its point. We salute you and ask that you let us tell the world your story." I then asked Meena for a pin and joyfully placed it on Daniel's lapel. We photographed this first-time event.

Become a bumblebee by telling us your story of personal triumph when others said it couldn't be done. Your personal story of achievement will empower others to do the same. We want to share it with others. The more that people see that anything *is* possible the more that it *will* be possible. Catch the buzz.

Tell us your story. Become a bumblebee.

33

It Has Been My Intent...

"The only thing we have to fear is fear itself."
—President Franklin Delano Roosevelt, the day
after the Japanese sneak attack on Pearl Harbor.

It has been my intent to remove your fear of—and to familiarize you with—modern dentistry. Marketers are experts at making people acquainted with certain products. They know that the more you see or hear of their product, the more likely you are to accept it.

My most earnest desire is to have made you familiar with what dentistry can provide you today. So many people have unrealistic perceptions regarding their dental fear. In *Profiles in Dental Courage*, I revealed how many people resolved their fears and moved on with their lives. You can do it, too. It is within your reach.

At this point, you should feel comfortable calling my team to discuss your needs. You are now armed with all the knowledge and strength you need to accomplish the impossible. Good oral health is intimately linked to good general health. Don't deny yourself the benefits of optimal well-being.

I have enjoyed spending this time with you. Believe me when I tell you that I have heard your comments as you have been reading these chapters. I have been hearing them for more than forty years. I am so convinced that you now have the ability to master your fear of dentistry that I will make this offer to you. Call my office for a complimentary consultation on your dental issues, and we *will* work them out once and for all. Just mention that you have read *Profiles in Dental Courage,* and you will be given the keys to open your mental prison door to set yourself free.

Good luck and remember, May the Floss Be with You.

(Stop rolling your eyes!)

Postscript: Oh No! Not Me!

"It isn't until you come to a spiritual understanding of who you are—not necessarily a religious feeling, but deep down, the spirit within—that you can begin to take control."
—Oprah Winfrey

I promise you this is not a joke. I am in Atlanta with Marji and have just finished a weekend professional educational conference. My boys joined us. They participated in an amazing program of self-exploration while learning the fundamentals of achieving success in life. After the conference, I decided to take two days of vacation since school had finished for them. We went to Georgia's number one natural tourist attraction called Stone Mountain. It certainly lived up to its name. Back at the Atlanta Airport, I happened to chomp on a pretzel and found a piece of gravel in my mouth. Spitting it out revealed nothing more than the palatal cusp of my left second bicuspid.

So those of you who say that God works in mysterious ways now have their dreams fulfilled. This tooth had had a large filling in it for ten years. But in recent times I had been experiencing a mysterious pain in this area. Neither X-rays nor clinical examination revealed anything wrong. It took a pretzel to expose the culprit. As you might imagine, my mind was starting to diagnose and plan treatment for this problem. Let's see, a broken tooth with no means of support for a filling. It'll need root canal therapy followed by a post and core. This core will provide a head for a crown to sit on. What a true treat. I had never had one before. I asked my associate at the office to take an intraoral photograph, and then we figured out what to do.

As it turned out only a large filling was placed. The root canal treatment, post and core, and crown were not needed. I'm no different from you. We're all the same. We always tend to think that the worst, most invasive resolution to our problems will be needed. The significance of this realization is that it reminded me to always be kind and calm to my patients. There is always something to be gained from every experience, including a broken tooth.

Made in the USA
Lexington, KY
19 June 2017